MARKETING
5.0

PHILIP KOTLER
HERMAWAN KARTAJAYA
IWAN SETIAWAN

MARKETING
5.0

TECHNOLOGY FOR HUMANITY

WILEY

Published by John Wiley & Sons, Inc., Hoboken, New Jersey.
Published simultaneously in Canada.

For general information on our other products and services or for technical support, please contact our Customer Care Department within the United States at (800) 762-2974, outside the United States at (317) 572-3993 or fax (317) 572-4002.

Wiley publishes in a variety of print and electronic formats and by print-on-demand. Some material included with standard print versions of this book may not be included in e-books or in print-on-demand. If this book refers to media such as a CD or DVD that is not included in the version you purchased, you may download this material at **http://booksupport. wiley.com**. For more information about Wiley products, visit **www.wiley.com**.

Library of Congress Cataloging-in-Publication Data

Names: Kotler, Philip, author. | Kartajaya, Hermawan, 1947- author. |
   Setiawan, Iwan, author.
Title: Marketing 5.0 : technology for humanity / Philip Kotler, Hermawan
   Kartajaya, Iwan Setiawan.
Description: Hoboken, New Jersey : Wiley, [2021] | Includes index.
Identifiers: LCCN 2020046415 (print) | LCCN 2020046416 (ebook) | ISBN
   9781119668510 (hardback) | ISBN 9781119668572 (adobe pdf) | ISBN
   9781119668541 (epub)
Subjects: LCSH: Marketing. | Technology.
Classification: LCC HF5415 .K685 2021 (print) | LCC HF5415 (ebook) | DDC
   658.8—dc23
LC record available at https://lccn.loc.gov/2020046415
LC ebook record available at https://lccn.loc.gov/2020046416

COVER DESIGN: PAUL MCCARTHY
COVER ART: © OXYGEN | GETTY IMAGES

SKY10030967_110221

Marketing's purpose always is to enhance people's lives and contribute to the Common Good.

—Philip Kotler

To all Asians, especially my Asia Marketing Federation brothers and sisters. We at MarkPlus, Inc. are very proud to collaborate with Philip Kotler as a knowledge lab for many books since 1998, including the Marketing X.0 *series.*

—Hermawan Kartajaya

Dedicated to the loving memory of my mom, Shinta, and my daughter, Keyvlin, who passed away during the writing of this book. Thank you to my family—my dad, Setiawan, my sister, Sisca, my wife, Louise, and my son, Jovin—for their endless love and care.

—Iwan Setiawan

Contents

About the Authors

Philip Kotler is Professor Emeritus of Marketing at the Kellogg School of Management, where he held the S.C. Johnson & Son Professorship of International Marketing. The *Wall Street Journal* ranks him as one of the top six most influential business thinkers. The recipient of numerous awards and honorary degrees from schools worldwide, he holds an MA from the University of Chicago and a PhD from Massachusetts Institute of Technology, both in economics. Philip has an incredible international presence—his books have been translated into more than 25 languages and he regularly speaks on the international circuit.

Hermawan Kartajaya is the founder and Executive Chairman of MarkPlus, Inc., and is one of the "50 Gurus Who Have Shaped the Future of Marketing," according to the Chartered Institute of Marketing, United Kingdom. Hermawan is also a recipient of the Distinguished Global Leadership Award from the Pan-Pacific Business Association at the University of Nebraska–Lincoln. He is also Chairman of the Asia Council for Small Business and a co-founder of the Asia Marketing Federation.

Iwan Setiawan is Chief Executive Officer of MarkPlus, Inc., where he helps businesses design their corporate and marketing strategies. A frequent writer and speaker, Iwan is also Editor-in-Chief of *Marketeers*. Iwan holds an MBA from the Kellogg School of Management at Northwestern University and a BEng from the University of Indonesia.

Acknowledgments

The authors would like to thank the leadership team at MarkPlus, Inc., who spent countless hours brainstorming with the authors: Michael Hermawan, Jacky Mussry, Taufik, Vivie Jericho, Ence, Estania Rimadini, Yosanova Savitry, and Edwin Hardi.

A very special thank-you to Richard Narramore at Wiley for his vision and continuous commitment to the *Marketing X.0* series. Without Richard, the books would not be possible. We would also like to thank the editorial team at Wiley—Deborah Schindlar, Victoria Anllo, Linda Brandon—for a great collaboration during the development of *Marketing 5.0*.

PART I

Introduction

CHAPTER 1

Welcome to Marketing 5.0

Technology for Humanity

We wrote our first book in the series, *Marketing 3.0: From Products to Customers to the Human Spirit*, in 2009. The book has since been published in 27 language editions around the world. As the subtitle suggests, the book describes the major shifts from product-driven marketing (1.0) to customer-oriented marketing (2.0) to human-centric marketing (3.0).

In Marketing 3.0, customers look for not only functional and emotional satisfaction but also spiritual fulfillment from the brands they choose. Thus, companies build differentiation with their values. Their products and operations aim not only to bring profits but also to provide solutions to the world's toughest social and environmental problems.

It took nearly 70 years for marketing to evolve from its product orientation to the concept of human centricity. During the decades of evolution, several marketing concepts have stood the test of time. Despite being "traditional" in nature, the segmentation-targeting-positioning concept as well as the product-price-place-promotion (4Ps) model have become universal staples for modern marketers globally.

We have always considered Marketing 3.0 to be the ultimate stage of traditional marketing. The entire building blocks of serving customers intellectually (1.0), emotionally (2.0), and spiritually (3.0) were complete. Although published a decade ago, the book's relevance has become more evident in today's era dominated by Generation Y and Generation Z populations. Genuinely caring for the society, the youth essentially forced companies to adopt social impact in the business model.

Marketing 4.0: The Pivot to Digital

When we wrote the next book in the series, *Marketing 4.0: Moving from Traditional to Digital*, in 2016, we pivoted to "digital" as the subtitle implies. In the book, we differentiated "marketing in the digital world" from digital marketing. Marketing in the digital world does not rely solely on digital media and channels. The digital divide still exists; thus, marketing requires an omnichannel—online as well as offline—approach. The concept is partly inspired by Industry 4.0—a high-level strategy of the German government—in which physical-digital systems are used in manufacturing sectors.

Although the use of technologies in Marketing 4.0 is fairly basic, the book introduced new marketing frameworks to serve customers in the hybrid—physical and digital—touchpoints across their customer journeys. It has thus far been published in 24 language editions worldwide and inspired companies to adopt fundamental forms of digitalization in their marketing activities.

The applications of marketing technology (martech), however, are so much more than just distributing content in social media or building an omnichannel presence. Artificial intelligence (AI), natural language processing (NLP), sensor technology, and the Internet of Things (IoT) have great potential to be game-changing for marketing practices.

We excluded these technologies in Marketing 4.0 as they were not yet mainstream at the time we wrote the book. And we believe marketers were still in the transitional and adaptation period to a digital world. But the COVID-19 pandemic has indeed accelerated the digitalization of businesses. With lockdowns and physical distancing policies in place, both the markets and marketers were forced to adapt to the new touchless and digital realities.

That is why we think this is the right time for *Marketing 5.0: Technology for Humanity*. It is time for companies to unleash the full power of advanced technologies in their marketing strategies, tactics, and operations. This book is also partly inspired by Society 5.0—a high-level initiative of Japan—which contains a roadmap to create a sustainable society supported by smart technologies. We agree that technology should be leveraged for the good of humanity. Marketing 5.0, therefore, has the elements of both the human-centricity of Marketing 3.0 and the technology-empowerment of Marketing 4.0.

It's Time for Marketing 5.0

Marketing 5.0 materializes against the backdrop of three major challenges: generation gap, prosperity polarization, and the digital divide. It is the first time in history that five generations living together on Earth have contrasting attitudes, preferences, and behaviors. The Baby Boomers and Generation X still hold most of the leadership positions in businesses and the highest relative buying power. But the digital-savvy Generations Y and Z now form the largest workforce as well as the biggest consumer markets. The disconnect between the older corporate executives who make most decisions and their younger managers and customers will prove to be a significant stumbling block.

Marketers will also face chronic inequality and imbalanced wealth distribution, which causes the markets to polarize. The upper class with high-paying jobs is growing and fueling the luxury markets. At the other end, the bottom of the pyramid is also expanding and becomes a large mass market for low-priced, value products. The middle market, however, is contracting and even vanishing, forcing industry players to move up or down to survive.

Moreover, marketers must solve the digital divide between people who believe in the potential that digitalization brings and those who do not. Digitalization brings fear of the unknown with the threats of job losses and concerns of privacy violations. On the other hand, it brings the promise of exponential growth and better living for humanity. Businesses must break the divide to ensure that technological advancement will move forward and not be welcomed with resentment. These challenges that marketers face in implementing Marketing 5.0 in the digital world will be the subject of Part 2 of the book (Chapters 2–4).

What Is Marketing 5.0?

Marketing 5.0, by definition, is the application of human-mimicking technologies to create, communicate, deliver, and enhance value across the customer journey. One of the critical themes in Marketing 5.0 is what we call the next tech, which is a group of technologies that aim to emulate the capabilities of human marketers. It includes AI, NLP, sensors, robotics, augmented reality (AR), virtual reality (VR), IoT, and blockchain. A combination of these technologies is the enabler of Marketing 5.0.

For many years, AI has been developed to replicate human cognitive abilities, especially to learn from unstructured customer data and discover insights that might be beneficial for marketers. When mixed with other enabling technologies, AI can also be utilized to provide the right offers to the right customers. Big data analytics enables marketers to personalize their marketing strategy to each customer—a process known as "segments of one" marketing. Today, such a practice is becoming more mainstream than ever.

Consider these examples of Marketing 5.0. With AI's machine learning, companies can envision if a new product with specific features is likely to succeed with the assistance of a predictive algorithm. Hence, marketers can skip many steps in the new product development process. In most cases, these predictions have better accuracy than backward-looking market research and produce insights faster than the time-consuming concept tests. PepsiCo, for instance, regularly launches beverage products based on in-depth analysis of customer conversations on social media.

AI can also help reveal shopping patterns useful for e-retailers to recommend the right products and content to a cluster of shoppers based on their profiles. The recommendation engines are the critical differentiation of e-commerce players and other digital businesses such as Amazon, Netflix, and YouTube. They continuously analyze past purchase histories to create a dynamic segmentation and profiling of the customers and find the hidden relationships between seemingly unrelated products to upsell and cross-sell.

Some companies across industries such as AB InDev, Chase, and Lexus leverage AI to develop advertising with minimum involvement of human personnel. AB InDev, the company behind Budweiser and Corona, monitors how various ad placements are performing and feeds the resulting insights to the creative team to generate more effective ads. Chase opted for an AI engine instead of a human copywriter to write ad copies for its digital banners. Lexus analyzed award-winning campaigns for the past 15 years, especially in the luxury markets, to create a television ad for the new ES sedan. With a script entirely written by AI, the company hired an Oscar-winning director to shoot the commercial.

The implementation of Marketing 5.0 is not just limited to back-office operations. Combined with NLP, sensors, and robotics, AI can assist marketers in performing customer-facing activities. One of the most popular applications is for customer service chatbots. Facing human resources challenges such as an aging society and rising costs, several companies also use robots or other automated means to replace frontline staff. Nestle in Japan, for instance, employs AI-empowered robots as coffee waiters. Hilton in the United States experiments with a robot concierge while Tesco in the UK aims to replace the cashiers with face-recognizing cameras.

With sensors and IoT, retailers can replicate the digital experience in the brick-and-mortar space. A face-detecting screen in a retail store, for instance, can estimate a shopper's demographic and offer the right promotions. Walgreens' digital coolers are an example of this. Augmented reality apps, such as the ones Sephora or IKEA use, allow shoppers to try on products before committing to buying them. Macy's and Target apply sensor technologies for in-store wayfinding as well as targeted promotion.

Some of these applied technologies might sound far-fetched and even intimidating for marketers. But we are beginning to see how affordable and accessible these technologies have become in recent years. An open-source artificial intelligence platform from Google and Microsoft is readily available for businesses. There are plenty of choices for cloud-based data analytics, accessible via monthly subscriptions. Marketers can also choose from a wide variety of user-friendly chatbot-builder platforms that even nontechnology persons can use.

We explore Marketing 5.0 from a high-level strategic perspective. We will cover the know-how of using advanced martech to a certain extent, but this is not a technical book. Our principle is that technology should follow strategy. The concepts in Marketing 5.0 are, thus, tools-agnostic. Companies can implement the methods with any supporting hardware and software available in the market. The key is that those companies must have marketers who understand how to design a strategy that applies the right technology for various marketing use cases.

Despite the in-depth discussion on technology, it is important to note that humanity should remain the central focus of Marketing 5.0. The next tech is applied to help marketers to create, communicate, deliver, and enhance value across the customer journey. The objective is to create a new customer experience (CX) that is frictionless and compelling (see Figure 1.1). In achieving it, companies must leverage a balanced symbiosis between human and computer intelligence.

AI has the capability of discovering previously unknown patterns of customer behavior from piles of data. Despite its computational power, however, only humans can understand other

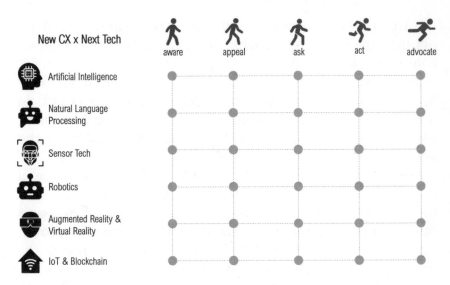

FIGURE 1.1   The Next Tech Across the New Customer Experience (CX)

humans. Human marketers are required to filter and interpret underlying motives for customer actions (see Figure 1.2). The reason for this is because human intelligence is highly contextual yet fuzzy. Nobody knows how seasoned marketers

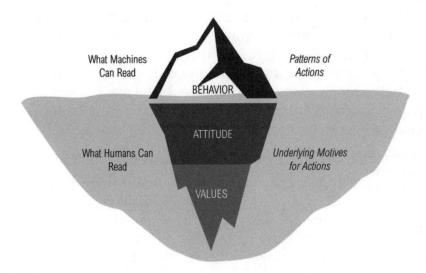

FIGURE 1.2   How Humans Add Value to Tech-Driven Marketing

extract insights and develop wisdom. And technologists have not managed to build a machine that can make a human-level connection with customers.

Since we cannot teach computers the things we do not know how to learn, the role of human marketers is still critical in Marketing 5.0. The central discussion in Marketing 5.0, hence, is around selecting where machines and people might fit and deliver the most value across the customer journey.

Part 3 of this book will discuss this in detail and is useful to give the right foundations for marketers before delving into the tactical applications. Chapter 5 helps companies assess their readiness for the use of advanced digital tools. Moreover, Chapter 6 will help marketers familiarize themselves with the next tech as the chapter contains a primer on the subject. Finally, Chapter 7 discusses a complete list of use cases that are proven across the new CX.

How Technology Can Enhance Marketing

The rise of social media marketing and search engine marketing as well as the exponential growth of e-commerce have introduced marketers to the benefits of digitalization. But marketing in the digital context is not much more than migrating customers to digital channels or spending more on digital media. Digital technology can revolutionize how marketers ply their trade. There are five ways technology can boost marketing practices:

1. **Make more informed decisions based on big data.**

   The greatest side product of digitalization is big data. In the digital context, every customer touchpoint—transaction, call center inquiry, and email exchange—is recorded. Moreover, customers leave footprints every time they browse the Internet and post something on social media. Privacy concerns aside, those are mountains of insights to extract. With such a rich source of information, marketers can now profile the customers at a granular and individual level, allowing one-to-one marketing at scale.

2. **Predict outcomes of marketing strategies and tactics.**

   No marketing investment is a sure bet. But the idea of calculating the return on every marketing action makes marketing more accountable. With artificial intelligence–powered analytics, it is now possible for marketers to predict the outcome before launching new products or releasing new campaigns. The predictive model aims to discover patterns from previous marketing endeavors and understand what works, and based on the learning, recommend the optimized design for future campaigns. It allows marketers to stay ahead of the curve without jeopardizing the brands from possible failures.

3. **Bring the contextual digital experience to the physical world.**

   The tracking of Internet users enables digital marketers to provide highly contextual experiences, such as personalized landing pages, relevant ads, and custom-made content. It gives digital-native companies a significant advantage over their brick-and-mortar counterparts. Today, the connected devices and sensors—the Internet of Things—empowers businesses to bring contextual touchpoints to the physical space, leveling the playing field while facilitating seamless omnichannel experience. Sensors enable marketers to identify who is coming to the stores and provide personalized treatment.

4. **Augment frontline marketers' capacity to deliver value.**

   Instead of being drawn into the machine-versus-human debate, marketers can focus on building an optimized symbiosis between themselves and digital technologies. AI, along with NLP, can improve the productivity of customer-facing operations by taking over lower-value tasks and empowering frontline personnel to tailor their approach. Chatbots can handle simple, high-volume conversations with an instant response. AR and VR help companies deliver engaging products with minimum human involvement. Thus, frontline marketers can concentrate on delivering highly coveted social interactions only when they need to.

5. Speed up marketing execution.

The preferences of always-on customers constantly change, putting pressure on businesses to profit from a shorter window of opportunity. To cope with such a challenge, companies can draw inspiration from the agile practices of lean startups. These startups rely heavily on technology to perform rapid market experiments and real-time validation. Instead of creating products or campaigns from the ground up, businesses can build on open-source platforms and leverage co-creation to accelerate go-to-market. This approach, however, requires not only the backing of technology but also the right agile attitude and mindset.

Five Components of Marketing 5.0

In essence, technology will enable marketing to be data-driven, predictive, contextual, augmented, and agile. Based on the ways advanced technology adds value to marketing, we define the five fundamental components of Marketing 5.0. Marketing 5.0 centers around three interrelated *applications*: predictive marketing, contextual marketing, and augmented marketing. But those applications are built on two organizational *disciplines*: data-driven marketing and agile marketing (see Figure 1.3). Part 4 is dedicated to exploring these five elements of Marketing 5.0.

Discipline 1: Data-Driven Marketing

Data-driven marketing is the activity of collecting and analyzing big data from various internal and external sources as well as building a data ecosystem to drive and optimize marketing decisions. This is the first discipline of Marketing 5.0: every single decision must be made with sufficient data at hand.

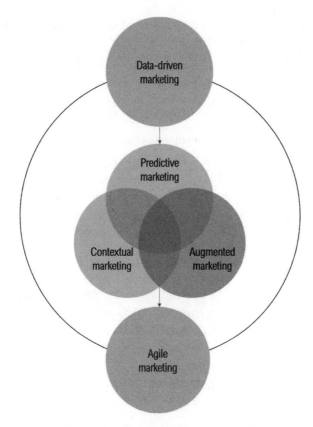

FIGURE 1.3   The Five Elements of Marketing 5.0

Discipline 2: Agile Marketing

Agile marketing is the use of decentralized, cross-functional teams to conceptualize, design, develop, and validate products and marketing campaigns rapidly. The organizational agility to deal with the ever-changing market becomes the second discipline that companies must master to ensure successful Marketing 5.0 implementation.

The two disciplines will sandwich the other chapters in Part 4. Data-driven marketing will be discussed in Chapter 8 while agile marketing will be explored in the concluding Chapter 12. We believe that for companies to run the three applications of

Marketing 5.0, they must start with building data-driven capability. In the end, what will truly make or break the implementation is the organization's agility in the execution.

Application 1: Predictive Marketing

Predictive marketing is the process of building and using predictive analytics, sometimes with machine learning, to predict the results of marketing activities before launch. This first application allows businesses to envision how the market will respond and proactively influence it. The concept will be reviewed in Chapter 9.

Application 2: Contextual Marketing

Contextual marketing is the activity of identifying and profiling as well as providing customers with personalized interactions by utilizing sensors and digital interfaces in the physical space. It is the backbone that allows marketers to perform one-to-one marketing in real-time, depending on the customer context. The concept will be explored in detail in Chapter 10.

Application 3: Augmented Marketing

Augmented marketing is the use of digital technology to improve the productivity of customer-facing marketers with human-mimicking technologies such as chatbots and virtual assistants. This third application ensures that marketers combine the speed and convenience of digital interface with the warmth and empathy of people-centric touchpoints. The concept will be discussed at length in Chapter 11.

The three applications are interconnected and hence are not mutually exclusive. Consider this example. Company X builds a predictive marketing model that forecasts what product a customer with a specific demographic will likely buy. For this model to work, the company must set up various sensors at the point of sales, which include a face recognition camera attached to a digital self-service kiosk. When a customer with the right demographic approaches the kiosk, the camera picks up a trigger and sends a signal to the screen to display a contextual ad offering the product recommended by the predictive model. The customer can also use the digital interface in a personalized manner. But at the same time, Company X also provides a frontline staff, augmented with digital tools containing the predictive model, with the ability to help the customer when the self-service option is not satisfactory.

Summary: Technology for Humanity

Marketing 5.0 is built upon the human-centricity of Marketing 3.0 and the technological prowess of Marketing 4.0. It is defined as the use of human-mimicking technologies to create, communicate, deliver, and enhance value in the overall customer experience. It starts by mapping the customer journey and identifying where marketing technologies (martech) can add value and improve the performance of human marketers.

Companies applying Marketing 5.0 must be data-driven from the get-go. Building a data ecosystem is the prerequisite to implementing the use cases of Marketing 5.0. It allows marketers to execute predictive marketing to estimate the potential return of every marketing investment. It also enables marketers to deliver personalized, contextual marketing to every individual customer at the point of sale. Finally, frontline marketers can design a seamless interface with the customers using augmented marketing. All these execution elements require corporate agility to provide a real-time response to market changes.

REFLECTION QUESTIONS

- Has the implementation of digital technologies in your organization gone beyond social media marketing and e-commerce?
- What are some of the advanced technologies that you envision will bring value to your organization?

PART II

Challenges Marketers Face in a Digital World

CHAPTER 2

Generation Gap

Marketing to Baby Boomers, X, Y, Z, and Alpha

A 25-year-old assistant marketing manager was assigned to design a print advertisement for a new product intended for Millennials. After conducting interviews with a sample of potential customers, she produced a beautiful ad with an eye-catching graphic and a one-line copy, followed by a website link as a call to action. What she did not anticipate was that her 50-year-old marketing manager complained about the lack of details on product features, advantages, and benefits on that print. Thinking that her manager did not understand the minimalistic marketing approach to Millennials, she quit her job—ironically confirming her manager's beliefs that younger staff could not accept criticism.

Today, this generational misalignment is happening in many organizations. Marketers around the world are facing the challenge of serving five different generations: Baby Boomers, Generation X, Generation Y, Generation Z, and Generation Alpha. The first four of these generations make up the workforce. The majority of Baby Boomers are still in the workforce. However, Generation X now holds most of the leadership roles globally. Generation Y is now the largest in the workforce, while Generation Z is the newest entrants. These generations have different levels of tech-savviness. Looking at the market through the generational lense will help marketers understand the best way to implement the tech-driven Marketing 5.0.

Challenges of Serving Different Generations

Every generation is shaped by a different sociocultural environment and life experience. Take, for instance, Generation X. Having either divorced or two working parents, they grew up with minimum parenting. As young adults, they were culturally influenced by MTV music videos. As a result, they value work–life balance more than other generations and are considered more independent and creative. As adults, they experienced the world without and with the Internet—allowing them to adapt well to both traditional and digital workplaces.

Every generation also has different preferences and attitudes toward products and services—prompting marketers to respond with a different offering, customer experience, and even business model. Generation Y, for instance, puts more priority on experience over ownership. They prefer using an Uber to owning a car. This preference has led to the rise of all kinds of on-demand services. Business models have also shifted from selling products to selling subscriptions. Generation Y prefers streaming on Spotify to buying a music album.

Despite understanding the distinctive needs of different generations, most companies are not well-positioned to serve all of them. Companies are often stuck with a rigid portfolio of products and services that does not allow customization toward every generation. It forces companies to serve only two or three generations at the same time. Companies also struggle to adapt to the shortened product lifecycle posed by the ever-changing needs and wants of younger generations. Many companies across industries—automotive, electronics, high tech, consumer packaged goods, and fashion—feel the pressure to quickly develop new products and make a profit in a narrow window.

Targeting also creates a dilemma since the most value is still being created when brands are serving Baby Boomers and Generation X—with their powerful resources and high willingness to pay. But most brand equity is being created when brands are being endorsed by Generations Y and Z—with their cool factor and digital savvy. And most importantly, Generations Y and Z are beginning to influence their Baby Boomer and Generation X parents in many purchase decisions. Companies need to balance between two goals: maximize value creation for the present and start positioning the brands for the future.

The Five Generations

We believe that every customer is unique, and with technological support, marketing will eventually be one-to-one—powered by customization and personalization at an individual level. In the future, marketers will serve segments of one, each with a unique set of preferences and behaviors. However, it is useful to see the overall direction of marketing evolution by looking at the mainstream market that companies will serve in the future. Understanding the collective demographic shift in the market is the most fundamental way to predict where marketing is heading.

The generational cohort is one of the most popular ways of mass-market segmentation. The premise is that people who were born and grew up within the same period experienced the same significant events. Thus, they share the same sociocultural experiences and are more likely to possess similar sets of values, attitudes, and behaviors. Today, five generational cohorts are living together: Baby Boomers, Generation X, Generation Y, Generation Z, and Generation Alpha (see Figure 2.1).

Baby Boomers: The Aging Economic Powerhouse

Baby Boomers were born between 1946 and 1964. The term *baby boom* refers to the high birth rate in the United States—and many other parts of the world—following the end of World War II. With postwar security and economy, many couples decided to have children, which became the prime target market for marketers at the time.

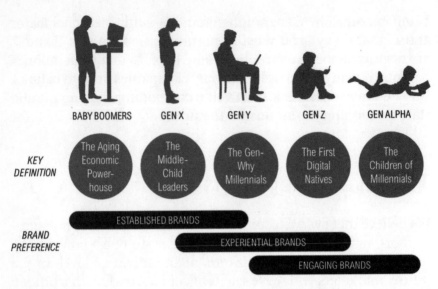

BABY BOOMERS   GEN X   GEN Y   GEN Z   GEN ALPHA

KEY DEFINITION

The Aging Economic Power-house | The Middle-Child Leaders | The Gen-Why Millennials | The First Digital Natives | The Children of Millennials

BRAND PREFERENCE

ESTABLISHED BRANDS

EXPERIENTIAL BRANDS

ENGAGING BRANDS

FIGURE 2.1   The Five Generations and Their Brand Preferences

The early Boomers, who were teenagers in the soaring 1960s, were raised in a relatively more affluent family. However, their adolescence was spent navigating through sociopolitical tensions during the decade. As a result, they are often associated with the counterculture movement in the United States and other Western countries. Many nonmainstream concepts such as social activism, environmentalism, and hippie lifestyle emerged during this era. The counterculture movement was further amplified by the rise of television and advertising as well as the New Hollywood wave.

Unlike the early Boomers, the late Boomers—also known as Generation Jones—were in economic distress by the time they were teenagers in the turbulent 1970s. Having working parents, they lived independently and worked harder in their early careers. This sub-generation within Baby Boomers was the precursor to Generation X—with whom they share many similar characteristics.

Due to its sheer size and the US postwar economic boom during their upbringing, Baby Boomers have become one of the major economic forces. For many decades, Baby Boomers had been the focus of marketers before Generation Y outnumbered them. Today, as they are living healthier and longer lives, more Baby Boomers delay retirement and extend their careers well beyond 65 years old. Still holding executive roles in corporations, Baby Boomers are often criticized by the younger generation for their unwillingness to adopt new technologies and break the conventional business wisdom.

Generation X: The Middle-Child Leaders

Generation X is a demographic group of people who were born between 1965 and 1980. Overshadowed and sandwiched by the popularities of Baby Boomers and Generation Y, Generation X has fallen off the radar among marketers and is thus dubbed the "forgotten middle child."

The Generation X cohort experienced the turbulent 1970s and the uncertain 1980s during their childhood and adolescence but entered the workforce in a better economic situation. They relate well with the concept of "friends and family." Growing up in either two-income or divorced families, Generation X children spent less time with their family and interacted more with their friends. The strong peer relationship within Generation X gave rise to the friendship portrayals in hit TV shows of the 1990s, such as *Beverly Hills 90210* and *Friends*.

As the middle-child cohort, Generation X experienced major consumer technology shifts, which influenced them to be highly adaptable. In their youth, Generation X grew up watching music videos on MTV and listening to mixtapes on their Walkman. In their adulthood, they experienced the use of CDs and MP3s as well as audio streaming to listen to music. They witnessed the rise and decline of DVD rentals and the shift to video streaming. Most importantly, their entry into the workforce was marked by the growth of the Internet—making them the early adopters of connectivity.

Although overlooked by most marketers, Generation X has become one of the most influential generations in the work-force today. With the average working experience of 20 years and strong work ethics, Generation X has held most leadership roles in business. Finding it harder to move up the corporate ladder with Baby Boomers extending their retirement, many of Generation X left their employers in their forties, started their own businesses, and became successful entrepreneurs.

Generation Y: The Gen-Why Millennials

Generation Y—those born between 1981 and 1996—has been the most talked-about cohort in the last few decades. Coming of age in the new millennium, they are widely known as Millennials. Born during another baby boom period, most of Generation Y are children of Baby Boomers. That is why they are also known as the Echo Boomer generation. In general, they are more well educated and culturally diverse than previous generations.

They are also the first generation who are strongly associated with the use of social media. Unlike Generation X, who first used the Internet in the workplace for professional reasons, Generation Y learned about the Internet at a much younger age. Thus, in the beginning, Generation Y embraced social media and other Internet-related technologies for personal goals.

On social media, they are very open to express themselves and often compare themselves to their peers. They feel the need to get validation and approval from their peers. As a result, they are heavily influenced by what their peers are saying and buying. They trust their peers more than established brands. Generation Y does a lot of online research and purchase, primarily on their mobile phones. But they do not buy products as much as older generations as they prefer experience over ownership. They do not focus on accumulating wealth and assets but on collecting life stories.

Due to their higher education, diversity, and exposure to unlimited content, Generation Y is more open-minded and idealistic. Generation Y questions everything, which makes them prone to workplace conflict with older generations who expect them to follow the norms.

Like their Baby Boomer parents, Millennials are often categorized into two sub-generations. The older Millennials—those born in the 1980s—entered the workplace during the 2008 global financial crisis and its aftermath, and therefore had to survive a tough job market. Some of them ended up building their own businesses. Due to very competitive work experience, they tend to have a clear separation between personal and professional lives. The younger Millennials—born in the 1990s—on the other hand, experienced a better job market. They tend to blend personal and professional lives. In other words, they only want jobs they enjoy—the work should be fulfilling.

The older sub-generation is a "bridge generation" because they learned to be adaptive to both the digital and physical world—just like the preceding Generation X. The younger sub-generation, however, is more like Generation Z. Because they adopted the Internet at a very young age, they naturally see the digital world as a seamless extension of the physical world.

Generation Z: The First Digital Natives

Marketers are now turning their attention to Generation Z. The offspring of Generation X, Generation Z—also known as Centennials—is a cohort of people born between 1997 and 2009. Many of Generation Z witnessed the financial struggles of their parents and older siblings, and therefore are more financially conscious than Generation Y. They tend to save money and view economic stability as an essential factor in their career choices.

Born when the Internet had already become mainstream, they are considered the very first digital natives. Having no experience of living without the Internet, they view digital technologies as an indispensable part of daily life. They always connect to the Internet through their digital devices for learning, news updates, shopping, and social networking. They consume content continuously through multiple screens, even when they are in social situations. As a result, they see virtually no border between the online and offline worlds.

Empowered by social media, Generation Z records their everyday lives on social media in forms of photos and videos. But unlike Generation Y, who is idealistic, Generation Z is pragmatic. In contrast to Generation Y, who likes to post more polished and filtered images of themselves for personal branding, Generation Z prefers to portray authentic and candid versions of themselves. Therefore, Generation Z hates brands that broadcast imageries that are manufactured and too good to be true.

Because the willingness to share personal information is relatively higher in Generation Z than in older generations, they want brands to be able to deliver personalized content, offerings, and customer experiences. They also expect brands to provide them with the ability to control and customize how they consume products or services. Due to the sheer volume of contents that are targeted at them, Generation Z truly values the convenience of personalization and customization.

As with Generation Y, Generation Z is much concerned about social change and environmental sustainability. Due to their pragmatism, Generation Z is more confident in their roles to drive change through their everyday decisions. They prefer brands that put a strong emphasis on solving social and environmental issues. They believe that their brand choices force companies to improve their sustainability practices. Generation Z is also passionate about making a difference through volunteering and expects its employers to provide the platform that enables this.

Generation Z also seeks for constant engagement throughout the relationship with brands. They expect brands to be equally stimulating as their mobile and gaming devices. Thus, they hope companies always renew their offers. They want companies to provide new interactive customer experiences at every touchpoint. Failure to meet this expectation results in low brand loyalty. Companies that target Generation Z must deal with this shortened product lifecycle.

Today, Generation Z has already outnumbered Generation Y as the largest generation globally. By 2025, they will make up most of the workforce and thus become the most significant market for products and services.

Generation Alpha: The Children of Millennials

Generation Alpha consists of those born from 2010 to 2025, which makes them the very first 21st-century children. Coined by Mark McCrindle, the Greek alphabet name signifies an entirely new generation that will be shaped by technological convergence. Not only are they digital natives, but they are also heavily influenced by the digital behaviors of their parents (Generation Y) and older siblings (Generation Z). Suitably, the launch of the first iPad—the device that most children are attached to—marked the emergence of this generation in 2010.

The characters of Generation Alpha are very much shaped and influenced by the parenting style of their Generation Y parents. Getting married at an older age, Generation Y put greater emphasis on parenting and children's education. They also teach their children about money and finance very early. Moreover, they raise their children in a very diverse and fast-paced urban environment. Therefore, Generation Alpha is not only well educated and tech-savvy but also inclusive and social.

Raised by Generation Y and influenced by Generation Z, Generation Alpha has been actively consuming content on mobile devices since childhood. Having relatively longer screen time than previous generations, Generation Alpha watches online videos and plays mobile games daily. Some have their own YouTube channels and Instagram accounts—created and managed by their parents.

Generation Alpha is more open to branded content, such as toy review channels on YouTube. Their learning style is more hands-on and experimental. They are very comfortable playing with tech toys, smart devices, and wearables. They see technology not only as an integral part of their lives but also as an extension of themselves. Generation Alpha will continue to grow up adopting and using human-mimicking technologies such as artificial intelligence, voice command, and robots.

Today, Generation Alpha does not yet have tremendous spending power, but they already have a strong influence on the spending of others. Google/Ipsos research reveals that 74% of Millennial parents involve their Generation Alpha children in household decisions. Moreover, some children have become social media influencers who are role models for other children. A report by Wunderman Thompson Commerce shows that 55% of children in the United States and UK would like to buy things that their social influencers use. Hence, it is only a matter of time before they become the focus of marketers globally.

The Life Stages of the Five Generations

Understanding what is essential for the five generations requires analyzing the life stages that they go through. In general, there are four life stages in human development, namely Fundamental, Forefront, Fostering, and Final (see Figure 2.2). Each life stage typically spans around 20 years, and when one grows into the next step, the life goals and priorities change significantly.

The first life stage is the Fundamental stage, in which the focus is on learning. During the first 20 years of life, one is still exploring and adapting to the environment. One learns

FUNDAMENTAL   FOREFRONT   FOSTERING   FINAL

LIFE STAGES

- Exploring and adapting to environment
- Learning and developing life skills
- Discovering personal identity

- Taking risks and pursuing dreams
- Making a living and building a career
- Developing committed romantic relationship

- Embracing parenthood and family life
- Mentoring and leading people at work
- Contributing back to society

- Maintaining health and social relationships
- Imparting wisdom to younger generations
- Enjoying life and staying happy

FIGURE 2.2   Human Life Stages and Key Priorities

knowledge and skills not only from formal education but also from friendship and social relationships. This stage is also about the new search for one's identity and reason for being.

The second stage is called the Forefront stage. During the second 20-year period, one starts to transition from learning to work. Starting to make a living and building a career, one becomes more independent. As health is at its peak during this stage, one is more willing to take risks and explore life to the fullest. One also starts to commit to a romantic relationship during this stage.

Entering the third stage of life or the Fostering stage, one begins to settle down and builds a family. One tends to return to a healthier lifestyle after a period of increased stress during the second life stage. More time is also being spent to nurture others. At home one focuses on parenthood and family life while at work one emphasizes mentoring and coaching younger generations. Contributing back to society also becomes a key life goal during this stage of life.

In the final stage, one tries to adapt to old age and to stay happy. This period is mostly about managing declining health and social relationships. One focuses on enjoying life by embarking on meaningful and fulfilling activities. Full of reflections on life lessons, one begins to develop wisdom and aims to impart what they've learned to younger generations.

For Baby Boomers, it typically takes 20 years to move from one stage to the next. Today, most Boomers are at the Final stage and are delaying retirement to remain active and ensure fulfilling lives. Generation X follows a fairly similar path in their life stages. Most of them are now in the Fostering life stage. Many become successful founders of startups and lead new businesses in their early 40s. They focus on work–life balance while at the same time contributing back to society.

Generation Y follows a slightly different path. They reach traditional life milestones such as marriage and childbirth at a much older age. It is a tradeoff as they reach other major life milestones, especially in career and societal contributions, at a much younger age. Generation Y is not willing to climb the traditional corporate ladder at the same pace as Baby Boomers and

Generation X. They want to catapult their way to the top by frequently changing jobs or starting their own business at a young age. As a result, they progress from one life stage to the next at a faster speed compared to Baby Boomers. Today, they are supposedly still in the Forefront stage, but some already have the mindset of the Fostering stage. They think about work–life balance at a much younger age. Their leadership style is based on empowering others through coaching and is driven by social purpose. Although their lives are surrounded by technology, Generation Y will put more emphasis on human-to-human interaction, which is the cornerstone of the Fostering life stage.

We believe that Generation Z and Generation Alpha also have shorter life stages, and therefore embrace more mature mindsets at a younger age. They are more willing to take risks and learn by doing—essentially merging the Fundamental and Forefront stages. They have a more significant desire to contribute to society even when they are still under 20 years old. Their perspective on technology is not shallow; they do not see technology as a mere gimmick. They see it as an essential enabler to do things quickly and accurately so that they can focus on what truly matters.

These shorter life stages have profound implications for the marketing approach. To serve Generation Z and Generation Alpha—the two most important generations in the next decade—it is not just about the application of technology. Instead, it is about how to use technology to enable human-centric solutions.

Generation Gap and Marketing Evolution

We always believe that marketing should be rewritten as *market-ing* as it continuously evolves to adapt to the ever-changing market (see Figure 2.3).

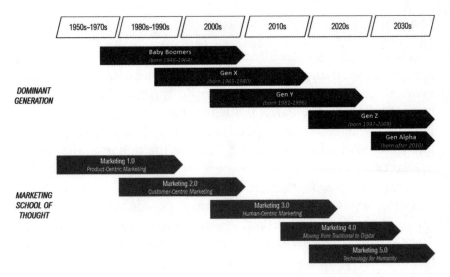

FIGURE 2.3   The Five Generations and Marketing Evolution

Marketing 1.0: Product Centric

Marketing 1.0 or product-centric marketing, which began in the United States in the 1950s, was primarily developed to serve the wealthy Baby Boomers and their parents. The main objective is to create the perfect products and services which produce the highest value in the minds of the customers. The winning products and services were the ones with full features and advantages over competitors. Having the best benefits for the customers, companies demand higher prices for these products and services over a long period. Thus, the essential marketing concepts created during this era focused on product development and life-cycle management as well as creating the best Four *P*s (product, price, place, and promotion). Customer satisfaction became the primary goal.

The biggest drawback of the Marketing 1.0 era, however, was that companies often make consumers consume what they do not need, which in turn created the culture of consumerism.

Marketing 2.0: Customer Centric

Following the counterculture—and anti-consumerism—movements between the mid-1960s and the mid-1970s, marketing evolved into a more customer-centric formula. It was further strengthened by the early 1980s recession, which led to significantly lower consumer spending power. The frugality of the late Boomers and Generation X became the major challenge for marketers.

Thus, in this Marketing 2.0 era, it centered around understanding segmentation, targeting, and positioning. Companies no longer created the perfect products and services for everyone. They learned more about their target market and sharply defined their market positioning. Companies removed bells and whistles and focused on select product features based on consumer needs and wants. It was reflected in the right level of pricing for the intended target market.

Companies also made a stronger effort to build a relationship with customers over time. Marketers applied the customer relationship management approach to retain customers and prevent them from switching to competitors. The objective shifted from customer satisfaction to retention.

Marketing 3.0: Human Centric

The rise of Generation Y—and the global financial crisis—in the late 2000s prompted another significant evolution of marketing. Empowered by the free access to information and disturbed by the financial industry scandals, Generation Y had a low level of trust toward corporations with profit-only motives. Generation Y demanded that companies create products, services, and cultures that bring positive societal and environmental impact. Thus, the era of human-centric marketing or Marketing 3.0 emerged. Companies began to embed ethical and socially responsible marketing practices into the business model.

Marketing 4.0: Traditional to Digital

Digitalization further complements the trend toward human centricity. Generation Y—and to a certain extent, Generation Z—gravitates toward a digital economy. The rise of mobile Internet, social media, and e-commerce changed the customer path to purchase. Marketers adapted to this change by communicating and delivering products and services through an omnichannel presence. They started to move from traditional to digital and implement Marketing 4.0.

Marketing 5.0: Technology for Humanity

With the rise of Generation Z and Generation Alpha, it is time for marketing to evolve once more.

The primary interest and concern of these two youngest generations aim in two directions. The first is to bring positive changes to humanity and improve the quality of human lives. The second is to drive technology advancement further forward in all aspects of humanity. To serve Generation Z and Generation Alpha, marketers need to continue to adopt the next technology to enhance human lives. In other words, Marketing 5.0 will be the integration between Marketing 3.0 (human centricity) and Marketing 4.0 (technology enabler).

Summary: Marketing to Baby Boomers, X, Y, Z, and Alpha

In the next decade, Generation X will hold almost all leadership positions in the marketing world. As marketers, they are the only generation to have embraced Marketing 1.0, Marketing 2.0, Marketing 3.0, and Marketing 4.0 throughout different stages of their lives. Supported by middle managers from Generation Y, Generation X will be the one to spearhead company marketing initiatives to serve Generation Z and Generation Alpha.

These two youngest generations will be the catalysts for Marketing 5.0, which is an integration between Marketing 3.0 and Marketing 4.0. They have great concern about how technology can empower and enhance humanity: improve human lives and create happiness. Companies that can earn the trust of Generation Z and Generation Alpha will be able to win the competition in the era of Marketing 5.0.

REFLECTION QUESTIONS

- What generations does your organization serve today? Have you fully understood their preferences and behaviors?
- Is your organization well positioned for the future? In other words, are you preparing your organization to serve the digital natives— Generation Z and Generation Alpha?

CHAPTER 3

Prosperity Polarization

Creating Inclusivity and Sustainability for Society

*T**he Platform* is a dystopian thriller movie set in a tall prison tower with hundreds of floors. Two inmates are randomly paired on each floor. They are fed daily through a moving platform that serves various kinds of gourmet food, descending from top to bottom floor. Inmates on the upper levels can eat as much as they like and leave the rest to the lower levels. Due to the greed and selfishness of those on the top floors, most prisoners are scraping for leftovers. Past a certain level, no more food is left, starving people beneath.

There is a chance to solve the problem. Since prisoners are rotated to different floors every month, they experience both moments of indulgence and hunger. And they know there is enough food for everyone if they ration their meals. But because everyone is striving for survival at some point, nobody has empathy toward others. The story reflects the classic "Prisoner's Dilemma," in which individuals acting in their self-interest often do not produce the best possible outcome.

The movie has received critical acclaim because it carries a message that resonates. It symbolizes imbalances in society and the social ignorance that causes them. People at the top prosper while those at the bottom suffer. And most do not seem interested in closing the gap. The metaphor also reflects the sustainability challenge that we are facing, where current generations exploit the environment without thinking about what they will leave for future generations.

Indeed one of humanity's toughest challenges is the widening gap between the rich and the poor, making society extremely polarized in every facet of life. Discussions on gender equality, clean energy, and smart cities only seem prominent among the elites. Meanwhile, at the other end of the spectrum, people struggle to get out of poverty and have access to food, healthcare, and basic sanitation. Because of this, social change often fails to cross the chasm from the wealthy early adopters to the less prosperous masses.

Some argue that technology will level the playing field and make a better life accessible to all. But coming from years of research, most technology solutions are still expensive. Without proper intervention, technology innovation will be biased toward the rich, who have better access. Those with higher education and high-value jobs, for instance, would be able to prosper using automation while those at the other end would lose their jobs.

Today, the use of technology for humanity is still too concentrated at the top. Companies will understandably follow the money and introduce technology to segments that have business potential. Thus, artificial intelligence algorithms focus too much on mapping the behaviors of a select few and assume they are similar to the mass majority. Advanced technology tends to be irrelevant for most people. That needs to change. Improving the accessibility and relevancy of technology is imperative for Marketing 5.0 to work.

The Polarized Society

Businesses have generated tremendous wealth over the past several decades. The distribution of that wealth, however, has been unequal, pulling people in opposite directions. The middle segment slowly migrates, either climbing to the top or falling to

FIGURE 3.1   The Polarizing Society

the bottom of the pyramid. It changes the shape of the society from a normal distribution to an M-shaped one—as observed by William Ouchi and Kenichi Ohmae—where the greatest numbers of people are in the upper and lower classes. On each end, people have conflicting life priorities and ideologies, which set them at odds with each other (see Figure 3.1).

Polarization of Jobs

One of the primary factors causing wealth disparity is the diverging opportunity to capture wealth. It is inherent in the corporate structure that those at the top have more power to determine or negotiate their generous pay level. The Economic Policy Institute reported that over the past four decades, top corporate executive compensation has grown by more than 1,000%. Some would claim that the high level of pay is well-deserved as most compensations link to the growth of shareholder value. But others would argue that excessive compensation is a result of executive power and demand instead of a true reflection of real contribution and capability. Nevertheless, the growth of executive pay is almost 100 times the rate of average employees' pay, widening the prosperity gap.

Another factor is the varying abilities and skills to capture wealth. As reported by the Organisation for Economic Co-Operation and Development (OECD), both high-value, high-paying jobs and low-value, low-paying jobs are expanding while everything in the middle is contracting. Talent with in-demand skills—both in white-collar and blue-collar occupations—would have a higher chance of getting employment, albeit not necessarily with high pay level. The Bureau of Labor Statistics projected that technical jobs that are related to alternative energy, information technology, healthcare, and data analysis would be the fastest-growing in the next decade. Some of these jobs come with high compensation, but others offer meager wages. This wage differential makes the structure of employment become increasingly polarized.

Both globalization and digitalization make the job polarization even worse for developed countries like the United States. Globalization allows businesses to move low-skill jobs offshore while focusing on high-skill expertise to export to emerging countries. Similarly, digitalization, especially in manufacturing automation, causes repetitive jobs to disappear while increasing the demand for more high-tech occupations.

Polarization of Ideologies

The paradox of globalization is that it calls for economic inclusivity but does not create equal economies. It appears that globalization hurts as many countries as it helps. Many blame globalization as the culprit of inequality. Coping with the tension, people begin to take sides and gravitate toward polarized beliefs and worldviews. Some believe opening up to the borderless world will bring more value while others call for protectionism with more walls. As seen in the Brexit process and the presidency of Donald Trump, politicians seek to represent the more closed model and amplify the separation to grow their electoral appeal.

Identity politics is rising around the world as a direct impact. The side effect is that standpoints and decisions are now determined through the political identity lens but not necessarily for the common good. And often, emotions rather than facts are fueling the diverging conversations. The social media filter bubbles, along with the spread of hoaxes, exacerbate it further.

As a result, several key issues are becoming more polarizing than ever. Political affiliations drive primary concerns. The strategies to combat climate change and regulate healthcare costs, for instance, are considered more pressing issues for Democrats than Republicans. The economy and the policy against terrorism, conversely, are top priorities for Republicans. Even the definition of a perfect home also differs between partisans. According to Pew Research Center, most Democrats prefer a denser neighborhood with public facilities within walking distance while most Republicans prefer the opposite. More Democrats than Republicans also favor living in a more ethnically diverse community.

Polarization of Lifestyles

Polarization occurs not only in ideological and communal choices but also in lifestyle preferences. On one end, the minimalist movement is becoming more popular. Marie Kondo, a Japanese home decluttering advisor, rose to global prominence for advocating the minimalist approach to tidying up one's house. The idea behind minimalism is that living with less stuff lowers stress, releases burdens, and gives more freedom to pursue what truly matters.

Financial hardships brought by the COVID-19 pandemic and unemployment indeed force some people to live a frugal lifestyle. They put more emphasis on essential and less on discretionary spending. But even some affluent individuals, with higher purchasing power, choose a more modest lifestyle and avoid shopping excessively. Also conscious of their carbon footprint and empathetic toward global poverty, they opt to forgo the pursuit of material possessions. The way of life follows conscious consumption, sustainable clothing, and responsible traveling practices.

Contrastingly on the other end, the consumerist lifestyle is also on the rise. Some people desire to show off lavish lifestyles and indulgent buys. Although they exist across different socio-economic classes, most aspirants are coming from the middle class and emerging affluent segment.

Using social media as a benchmark tool, the consumerists aspire to emulate the people in the higher social tiers and climb up the ladder. Often the early adopters, they rush to buy newly launched products. Their social media feeds become a journal of brand experiences. The "fear of missing out" (FOMO) often haunts them and influences their buying decisions and life priorities. The mantra is "you only live once" (YOLO), so they go all out on spending.

People at both ends of the spectrum believe that their lifestyles bring them happiness. And both the consumerists and the minimalists attract marketers who aim to capitalize on the emerging lifestyles. In fact, they are now two of the biggest markets worth pursuing, as anything in between is disappearing.

Polarization of Markets

Markets no longer consist of a wide range of offerings from the cheapest to the most luxurious and have started to polarize between the top and bottom ends. The middle segment is disappearing as people either trade down to quality no-frill offerings or trade up to more premium luxury offerings. As a result, top and bottom players are growing while edging out the midmarket players, which are struggling to stay relevant. And it is happening across product categories: grocery and fashion retailers, food services, airlines, and automotive (see Figure 3.2).

Economic crises, especially the one accompanying the recent pandemic, seem to have a lasting impact on the spending of low-income customers. During difficult times, there had been a surge of discount shoppers. Customers tried basic, low-priced products to save money. They discovered that the quality was acceptable and had become accustomed to it. Some even realized that they had previously been overspending and would never go back to the higher-priced brands. This trend is coupled with recent quality improvements in low-cost products, which have been

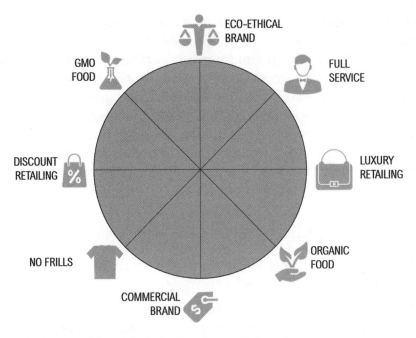

FIGURE 3.2   Market Polarization Across Categories

exceptional due to cheaper but more efficient manufacturing technology.

On the other side, higher-income customers were less prone to and even benefited from crises. The crises and the pandemic had reminded them of the importance of wellness and therefore led them to premium products and services that offer exactly that. It also remains true, especially for the newly rich, that earning more is often equal to spending more. Being affiliated to an exclusive community also encourages them to live similar lifestyles as their peers and show off their success. Thus, they will always aim to trade up to higher-tier offerings.

To adapt to the trend, industry players are pursuing either cost leadership or customer experience strategy. Low-cost providers focus on the intrinsic value of goods and services. It is about removing the bells and whistles and doubling down on the core benefits while convincing people of no quality compromise. They shift strategy away from bundled to unbundled value propositions and let customers pick and choose the product and service configurations that work for them.

Meanwhile, the premium-priced brands emphasize augmenting the extrinsic value of their offerings. Total-customer-experience innovation is the name of the game, providing customers with top-quality ingredients, exclusive sales and service channels, and luxury brand narratives all in one bundled package. They also attempt to grow their share by inviting more middle-tier customers to trade up by offering affordable luxury offerings.

Why Inclusivity and Sustainability Matter

The polarization of society, stemming from rising wealth disparity, may have a profound impact on many facets of human lives. The divide between people who are barely surviving and people who are thriving amid globalization and digitalization must not be ignored. Political uncertainty, social instability, and economic collapse are some of the significant risks if it remains unresolved. Businesses are partly responsible for the unequal distribution of wealth. The markets expect companies to be the ones fixing it with a more inclusive and sustainable approach to pursuing growth (see Figure 3.3).

The Sustainable Growth Imperative

Businesses have discovered in recent years that new pockets of growth were harder to find. Unserved markets with buying power have become rare. Even the best-run companies have struggled to create and sustain organic growth through both market expansion and new product introduction. And it will remain a formidable challenge. Economists have predicted that global economic growth will continue to slow down in the next decade.

Common hurdles such as market saturation, the proliferation of new entrants, weakened buying power, and overly complicated

FIGURE 3.3   The Reasons Behind Corporate Activism

operations might have contributed to the near-stagnancy. Nevertheless, it was perhaps a reminder that corporations would soon reach the limits of growth, not only from an ecological but also a societal point of view. The environment has a limited carrying capacity, and so does the market.

Businesses used to think that if they reinvested some of their profits for the development of society, they did it at the expense of faster growth. Companies must realize that the opposite is true. In doing business, negative externalities must be taken into account. Decades of aggressive growth strategies have left the environment degraded and society unequal. Companies cannot thrive in a failing and declining society.

If the emphasis is solely on growth—not development— businesses will quickly hit the limit. With prosperity polarization looming large, the market—especially the bottom half—will be bound to fail in absorbing more ambitious growth initiatives. Successful companies are the ones with large enough power to undo the damage. Hence for businesses to be sustainable, growth plans must include a key element of societal development.

From the future growth point of view, the social activism that companies conduct will prove a good investment. When billions of underserved people are out of poverty, become more educated, and earn a better income, the markets around the world substantially grow. The previously untapped segments become new sources of growth. Moreover, in a more stable society and a sustainable environment, the costs and risks of doing business are much lower.

The New Hygiene Factor

When Marketing 3.0 was introduced a decade ago, a purpose-driven business model was a relatively new source of differentiation that gave early adopters a competitive edge. As a group of customers began to favor brands whose activities had a positive social impact, a handful of companies started to embrace the human-centric approach and make it the core business strategy. These pioneering brands, such as The Body Shop and Ben & Jerry's, were considered cool. Several solutions to societal problems were embedded in their businesses, allowing customers to participate. Humanity's toughest challenges were, at the same time, the biggest business opportunities for these companies.

Today, this trend of human-centricity has become mainstream. Thousands of companies have put particular focus on their social and environmental impact, even actively using it as a major source of innovation. Many brands have captured a loyal following by promoting a health-conscious lifestyle, minimizing carbon footprint, conducting fair trade with emerging market suppliers, ensuring good labor practice, or building entrepreneurship at the bottom of the pyramid.

It has become a hygiene factor that without broader vision, mission, and values, brands have no license to compete. Companies that fail to incorporate responsible practices run the risk of being overlooked by prospective customers. Customers are increasingly making their buying decisions based on their perceptions of a company's ethical conduct. Indeed, customers now expect brands to work for the good of society at large, and corporations know it. The "Stop Hate for Profit" campaign, in which Microsoft, Starbucks, Pfizer, Unilever, and hundreds of other companies paused advertising on Facebook, calling for the social network's better handling of hate speech and misinformation, is a testament to the importance of corporate activism.

Brands should develop and nurture—not only exploit—the markets in which they are competing. In other words, businesses are considered responsible for growing not only short-term shareholder value but also long-term societal value. And thanks to the Internet, companies are under constant scrutiny, and it is easier for customers to monitor the ethical aspects of businesses. It is now standard practice for companies to monitor and publish their progress through sustainability reporting, which regularly discloses the economic, environmental, and social impacts caused by their operations.

The Push from Within

The external trends tend to mirror the internal dynamics as well. Social impact resonates well with the younger talent pool. Responding to the demands of their employees, companies begin to include a social mission in corporate values. Generation Y employees, the largest in the workforce, have been longtime promoters of social change. They exert influence not only by using their buying power as customers but also by championing social change from within. And now, Generation Z is starting to come into the workforce—soon taking over as the new majority—and the internal pressure for socially and environmentally responsible practice is escalating. (See Chapter 2 for information on the different generations.)

Diversity, inclusion, and equal opportunity in the workplace have become a must-have in a war for talent, significantly influencing the recruitment, remuneration, and people-development practices. And plenty of research from BCG, McKinsey, and Hays has shown that those practices indeed improve corporate productivity and financial performance through a healthier culture, better creativity, and a richer perspective.

Moreover, corporate values are more important than ever to attract and retain younger-generation employees. To become employers of choice, companies need to use the same story-telling narratives with their employees that they use with their customers. Corporate values feel most genuine when they are aligned with the business. For example, oil and gas companies must pay attention to the shift to renewable energy and electric vehicles. Personal care brands may choose to contribute to the hygiene and sanitation of communities that they serve. Eradicating obesity can be the focus of a food and beverage company.

But the credos can no longer be merely jargon; companies must show integrity and practice what they preach as employees can easily smell disingenuous promises and opportunistic acts. It should not stop at the level of charitable donations or philanthropic acts. Instead it must influence the entire business strategy, from the supply chain, product development, and distribution to human resource practices.

Aligning Strategies to Sustainable Development Goals

The role of business in improving society is critical. But even if most companies have invested their resources and put corporate activism at the heart of their strategies, the impact may not be adequate to change the world. Concerted actions are required to ensure synergistic outcomes. A global partnership platform involving governments, civil societies, and businesses will enable visionary companies to find like-minded organizations to collaborate with across the globe.

Here is where the Sustainable Development Goals (SDGs) play a crucial role. In 2015, United Nations member states introduced Agenda 2030 and pledged to achieve a comprehensive set of 17 goals known as the SDGs (see Figure 3.4). Replacing

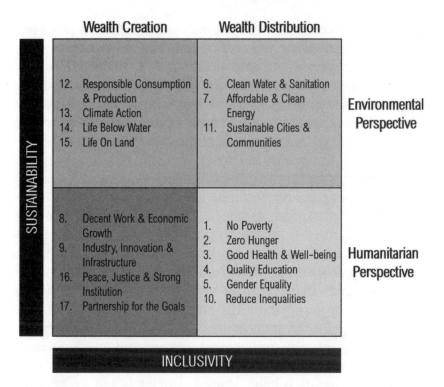

FIGURE 3.4   Inclusive and Sustainable Development in the 17 SDGs

the Millennium Development Goals (MDGs), they serve as a shared vision as well as a standard blueprint to guide key stakeholders in tackling the most pressing social and environmental challenges.

The implementation of SDGs still faces challenges down the road, primarily stemming from the low level of perceived relevance. Research commissioned by the World Economic Forum revealed that around 74% of global citizens are aware of SDGs. However, most of them are more inclined to support only urgently relevant goals, such as those related to food, water, health, and energy. And they start to disengage when it comes to more lofty goals, such as gender and income inequality.

The role of companies in improving this lack of affinity is apparent. By including the SDGs in their marketing and other business activities, companies can help make the goals integrate seamlessly into customer lives. It will make the SDGs more of a household name rather than a governmental initiative.

In a simplified way, companies can look at the SDGs from two broad perspectives: humanitarian and environmental. On the one hand, making the world a better place involves creating improved likelihood for the people on the planet—providing them with the primary necessities, fundamental life skills, and equal opportunities. On the other hand, it also involves preserving and protecting the environment—making it a sustainable home for future generations.

The SDGs also promote both the creation of wealth and the fair distribution of it. Specific goals aim to create perfect ecosystems and conditions for everyone to prosper. Developing a quality infrastructure and safe housing as well as reducing the crime rate and corruption are some examples of the targets. Other goals focus on uniformly spreading the opportunities to thrive, especially for marginalized groups. Examples include eliminating discrimination against women and ensuring equal access to education.

The categorization helps simplify the goals and assists companies in understanding and prioritizing how they can best contribute. Looking at the 17 goals can be a bit overwhelming and make people switch off. But in essence, the goals are simply about promoting inclusive and sustainable development. Thus, companies can quickly identify where they can make a real impact along their value chain.

On the inclusivity front, healthcare companies, for example, may focus on promoting healthy lifestyles and providing affordable diagnostic tools and medications to the rural poor. On the sustainability front, the companies may utilize technology and deliver telehealth services to remote areas that reduce mobility, conserve energy, and cut carbon emissions.

A financial services company may push for financial inclusion, targeting underserved markets and utilizing a financial technology (fintech) model. At the same time, they may embrace and facilitate sustainable investing, for instance, by funding the development of renewable energy while avoiding investment in environmentally degrading projects.

Manufacturing companies may contribute to sustainability by adopting the circular economy model that employs reduction, reuse, and recycling of production materials. They may also contribute to the inclusive economy by hiring minorities and involving small businesses in their supply chains.

Businesses may soon realize the direct and indirect benefits of adopting these inclusive and sustainable practices. Energy-efficient operations in offices and manufacturing facilities means costs will go down. The reduced mobility due to remote work and shared transport will also save some money for businesses.

Moreover, catering to the underserved opens up new market opportunities, and most importantly, forces companies to reverse-innovate. In the past, innovation usually has come from developed countries and trickled down to the developing nations. Today, it is the other way around. Companies such as GE, for example, have been creating low-cost medical equipment for developing countries and then marketing it to developed nations—repositioning it as "portable" devices.

Setting up clear targets for achievement is useful for companies to understand the scale and scope of their activism. It also allows companies to drive the implementation within their organizations. Measuring and monitoring the benefits will encourage companies to continue their practices. It makes it more evident that corporate activism is not only a responsibility but also a sound investment. Reporting the result and making it transparent, moreover, will inspire similar companies to follow suit and help potential partners identify possible collaboration.

Summary: Creating Inclusivity and Sustainability for Society

One of the main challenges marketers face today is the extreme polarization happening in every aspect of human lives, from jobs to ideologies to lifestyles to markets. The root cause is the widening gap between the top and bottom socioeconomic classes.

The middle market starts to disappear, either dropping down or going up.

When everything is polarized, there are only two meaningful ways to position your brands and companies. It limits the markets in which businesses can play. But most importantly, it limits growth opportunities, especially amid the slowing economy and the proliferation of players.

Inclusive and sustainable marketing—aligned with the sustainable development goals (SDGs)—solves the problem through a better redistribution of wealth, which in turn will return the society to its original shape. Companies must embed the concept in their business model, investing back into the society with purpose. And businesses must utilize technology as it will play a major role by accelerating the progress and opening up opportunities for everyone.

REFLECTION QUESTIONS

- Have you embraced the concept of human-centricity in your organization and included social impact in your vision, mission, and values?
- Think of how you can make more impact by aligning your strategies to the sustainable development goals (SDGs). Which of the 17 goals are related to your business?

CHAPTER 4

Digital Divide

Making Tech Personal, Social, and Experiential

In the April 2000 issue, *Wired* published an article titled "Why the Future Doesn't Need Us" by Bill Joy—a co-founder of Sun Microsystems. The article postulated a dystopian scenario whereby machines with superior intelligence would displace humans—known as the Singularity era. In that final year of the 20th century, *Wired* also released several other cover stories that explored the combination of robotics and artificial intelligence (AI) and predicted how those advanced technologies would impact the future of humanity.

After two decades, the predicted scenario has not yet materialized. The Singularity is still a matter of debate. Elon Musk of Tesla and Jack Ma of Alibaba famously had an argument on "human versus machine" at the World AI Conference stage in 2019. Elon Musk reiterated Bill Joy's concern that AI could end human civilization while Jack Ma maintained that humans would always be far superior to machines because of their emotional capacity.

Businesspeople have been wary of the threat of AI, from the loss of jobs to the extinction of humanity. But many wonder whether the danger is overrated. We imagined a long time ago futuristic AI-powered automation, such as fully automated smart homes, autonomous cars, and self-manufacturing 3D printers. But the automation has only made them available in forms of limited prototypes and has not managed to go mainstream.

Automation will indeed continue to take over some jobs. Brookings Institution predicted that automation threatens to replace 25% of jobs in the United States, especially the repetitive tasks. But AI has a long way to go to catch up with human intelligence and to replace it altogether. Even proponents of the Singularity believe that it will take a few more decades for it to happen. Ray Kurzweil of Google and Masayoshi Son of Softbank predicted that the Singularity would only come about by 2045–2050.

The Digital Divide Still Exists

There were close to 5 billion Internet users as of 2020. This number continues to grow at a rate of 1 million new users per day, as estimated by *We Are Social*. Thus, it will take us another decade to reach 90% penetration. By 2030, there will be more than 8 billion Internet users globally, which accounts for more than 90% of the world's population.

The fundamental barrier of connectivity is no longer the availability and accessibility of the Internet. Nearly the entire global population already lives within the mobile cellular network coverage. Take, for example, Indonesia. The fourth most populous nation on Earth has built over 216,000 miles of land and submarine fiber-optic network to provide high-speed Internet to people living in more than 17,000 islands, according to its Minister of Communication and Information Technology, Johnny Plate.

Instead, the primary hurdle is the affordability of access and the simplicity of use cases. And as Internet usage is not yet evenly distributed, the new users will come mostly from emerging markets. These markets are often mobile-first and mobile-only. Affordable mobile devices, lightweight operating systems, cheap data plans, and free Wi-Fi hotspots are vital drivers to acquire the "Next Billion Users" segment.

Aside from connecting people, the Internet also connects devices and machines—also known as the Internet of Things

(IoT). It can be utilized for monitoring purposes such as smart metering and asset tracking both in the household and industrial contexts. With the IoT, where devices and machines can communicate with one another, everything can be managed remotely and automatically without the need for human operators. Thus, ultimately, the IoT will be the backbone of automation, whereas AI becomes the brain that controls the devices and machines.

Although technology companies have forecasted hundreds of billions of connected IoT devices by 2030, the realization is slow. Gartner estimated only close to 6 billion IoT devices installed as of 2020, primarily in forms of smart electricity meters and building security surveillance. The key driver to grow this number is 5G— the fifth-generation mobile technology. 5G is up to 100 times faster and supports 10 times more devices than the current 4G network, which makes it much more efficient for the IoT.

The near-ubiquitous human-to-human and machine-to-machine connectivity is the fundamental infrastructure for a fully digital economy. It enables automation and remote manufacturing—making traditional supply chains obsolete. It allows for seamless interaction, transaction, and fulfillment among buyers and sellers. In the context of the workplace it creates better employee coordination and makes business processes more efficient—ultimately improving employee productivity.

But a fully digital infrastructure does not guarantee a fully digital society. Digital technologies are still being used primarily for basic communication and content consumption purposes. More advanced applications are still scarce, even in private sectors. To close the digital divide, both companies and their customers must increase their adoption of technologies.

Despite having the same access to digital infrastructure, adoption rates across industries vary. High-tech, media and entertainment, telecommunications, and financial services industries are some of the early adopters of digitalization. On the other hand, other sectors such as construction, mining, healthcare, and government are lagging.

Many factors influence the different willingness to implement digitalization. Incumbent market leaders often hesitate to replace accumulated physical assets with digital ones. But usually, an emerging competitor—a digital disruptor with less capital-intensive operations—forces their hand. Another driving force is the need to cut the workforce and other costs in the face of declining profitability. In industries with diminishing profit pools, the pressure to digitalize is more profound.

But the defining driver of digitalization is the push from customers. When customers demand digital channels for communications and transactions, companies will be obliged to comply. When customers highly value digital customer experience, the business case for investment will be justified. That way, the digital divide can be eliminated. A more digital market will lead to better marketing practices and allow companies to embrace Marketing 5.0.

The Perils and Promises of Digitalization

Traditionally, the digital divide refers to the gap between segments with access to digital technology and those without access. But the real digital divide is between the advocates and the critics of digitalization. There is a polarized view of whether a fully digital world brings more opportunities or more threats (see Figure 4.1). The digital divide will continue to exist unless we manage the risks and explore the possibilities.

Perils of Digitalization

There are five threats of digitalization that strike fear in the hearts of many people.

#1 Automation and Loss of Jobs As businesses incorporate automation technologies such as robotics and AI in their

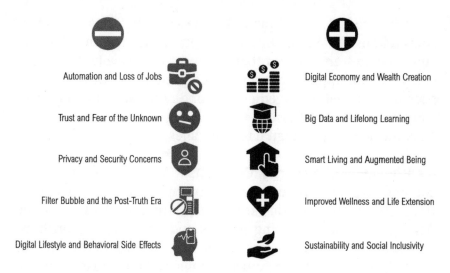

FIGURE 4.1   Perils and Promises of Digitalization

processes, there will be job losses. Automation aims to optimize productivity by using fewer resources and improving reliability. But not all jobs will be at risk. Repetitive tasks, which have low value and are prone to human errors, are the low-hanging fruit for robotic process automation (RPA). Jobs that require human empathy and creativity, however, are harder to displace.

The threat is also not equal globally. In developed countries, where labor costs are higher, the impact of automation on efficiency will be more significant. In emerging countries, on the other hand, the cost of implementing automation to replace human labor is still difficult to justify. These variations make the digital divide harder to close.

#2 Trust and Fear of the Unknown   Digitalization is becoming far more complicated than just connecting people through mobile devices and social media. It has crept into every facet of human lives, from commerce to mobility to education to healthcare. Fundamental to this complex digitalization is AI technology, which aims to not only imitate but also surpass human intelligence.

Advanced AI algorithms and models are often beyond human comprehension. When humans perceive a lack of control, it creates anxieties and causes them to react defensively. It is especially true for applications which require a high degree of trust, such as financial management, autonomous vehicles, and medical treatment. Trust issues will be a significant factor holding back the adoption of digital technologies.

#3 Privacy and Security Concerns AI feeds on data, and companies gather the data from customer databases, historical transactions, social media, and other sources. With the data, the AI engine creates profiling models and prediction algorithms, which allow companies to have an in-depth understanding of the customer's past and future behaviors. Some customers see the capability as a tool for customization and personalization. But others see it as an invasion of privacy for commercial gain.

Digital technology also poses a threat to national security. Autonomous weapon systems such as combat drones are harder to defend. When every aspect of human life is already digital, countries are more prone to cyberattacks. An attack on the IoT network could disable the entire digital infrastructure of a nation. Businesses and countries must overcome these privacy and security concerns, which remain a significant hurdle to technology adoption.

#4 Filter Bubble and the Post-Truth Era Both search engines and social media have overtaken traditional media as the primary source of information in the digital era. They hold power to shape perceptions and construct opinions. But there is one inherent problem with these tools: the use of algorithms that provide information tailored to users' profiles. The personalized search results and social media feeds end up reinforcing preexisting beliefs—creating polarized and extreme opinions.

More concerning is the emergence of a post-truth world where it is harder to differentiate between a fact and a lie. Disinformation is everywhere, from hoaxes to deep fakes. Utilizing the power of AI, it is easier to create fake audio and video that seem realistic. We need to manage this unintended consequence of technology to bridge the digital divide.

#5 Digital Lifestyle and Behavioral Side Effects   Mobile apps, social media, and gaming offer constant stimulation and engagement that glues people to their screens for hours. This addiction may prevent many people from building in-person interaction, doing physical activity, and having proper sleep habits—affecting their overall well being. Over time, too much screen time also shortens the attention span and makes it difficult to focus on productive tasks.

Digital technology also makes daily activities more convenient and effortless, from having groceries delivered to the doorstep to navigating the streets with Google Maps. It makes people dependent and complacent. When making decisions, we ignore our judgment and rely on what the AI algorithm suggests to us. We let machines do the work and make less intervention, creating what is known as the automation bias. Overcoming these behavioral side effects will be a significant challenge when making digitalization universal.

Promises of Digitalization

Despite the risks associated with it, digitalization unlocks tremendous possibilities for society. We list five scenarios in which digitalization brings value.

#1 Digital Economy and Wealth Creation   First and foremost, digitalization enables the rise of the digital economy, which creates massive wealth. Digitalization allows businesses to build platforms and ecosystems that process large-scale transactions without geographical and industry boundaries. Digital technologies empower companies to innovate not only the customer experience but also the business model. It helps companies meet customers' growing expectations, increase willingness to pay, and ultimately drive better value creation.

Unlike traditional models, digital business models require fewer assets, have faster time to market, and are highly scalable. Thus, it allows companies to achieve exponential growth in a short time. Digitalization across the customer experience also generates higher productivity and better profitability due to fewer errors and lower costs.

#2 Big Data and Lifelong Learning Digital platforms and ecosystems change how we do business. They seamlessly connect different parties—companies, customers, and other stakeholders—for limitless communications and transactions. Instead of amassing physical assets, these platforms and ecosystems across many industries collect a massive amount of raw data, which is the fuel for AI engines to create an extensive knowledge base.

The digital knowledge base will further accelerate the growth of Massive Open Online Courses (MOOCs) and enhance it with AI-powered training plans and teaching assistants. It will empower people to have lifelong learning of new skills to stay relevant in the AI era.

#3 Smart Living and Augmented Being Digitalization could realize the things that we have only seen in utopian movies. In a fully digitalized world, we will be living in a smart home where every action is either automated or voice-activated. A robot assistant will help with chores. The fridge is self-ordering, and a drone is delivering the groceries. Whenever we need anything, we will always 3D-print it. In the garage, an autonomous electric vehicle is on standby to take us wherever we want.

When it happens, the connector between us and the digital world will no longer be limited to our mobile phones. The interface will expand to smaller devices that are wearable and even implantable in human bodies—creating an augmented living. Elon Musk's Neuralink, for example, is developing a computer chip implant to create a brain–computer interface which allows humans to control computers with their mind.

#4 Improved Wellness and Life Extension   In the wellness space, advanced biotechnology aims to extend human life spans. Using big data in healthcare, AI will enable new drug discovery and precision medicine—with personalized diagnostics and treatments tailored to individual patients. Genomics will provide gene engineering capabilities to prevent and cure genetic diseases. Neurotechnology will edge closer to implanting a chip that treats brain disorders. Continuous health tracking with wearables or implantables will allow for preventive healthcare.

Moreover, similar progress is being made in food technology. A combination of biotechnology and AI intends to optimize food production and distribution to prevent hunger and malnourishment. We also see the rise of age-tech startups that provide products and services targeting aging populations to manage their longevity and improve quality of life.

#5 Sustainability and Social Inclusivity   Digitalization will also play a significant role in ensuring environmental sustainability. The sharing of electric vehicles will be one of the main drivers. The concept of peer-to-peer solar energy trading, which allows neighbors to share excess electricity, will also help energy conservation.

In manufacturing, AI will help reduce waste from design to material selection to production. With AI, we will establish a circular economy—a closed-loop system of continuous use of materials through reuse and recycle.

Upon closing the digital divide and reaching universal connectivity globally, we will create a truly inclusive society where we provide equal access to market and know-how for low-income communities. It will improve their livelihood and help end poverty.

The polarized view toward digitalization is the new digital divide. To end the debate, we need to dive deep into the human side of technology and leverage technology that brings out the best in humanity.

Technology Can Be Personal

In the Marketing 5.0 era, customers expect businesses to understand them and deliver personalized experiences. While it is feasible for companies with only a handful of customers, it is challenging to do it at scale and consistently. It is imperative to use technology to model specific customer profiles, generate tailored offers, provide customized content, and deliver personalized experiences.

AI uplifts every touchpoint across the customer path in three ways. First, it enables smarter targeting: delivering the right offers at the right moments and to the right customers. Second, it ensures a better product fit. Companies may provide personalized products and even allow customers to customize their products. Finally, it allows for better engagement. Companies can deliver tailored content and interact more intimately with customers.

Using AI for personalization improves customer satisfaction and loyalty and in turn increases customer acceptance toward data sharing. If the actual benefits of personalization outweigh the threat of privacy violations, customers will be more willing to share personal data. The key is to embrace selective human attention and create perceived control. Customers find personalization more agreeable if it makes their decision making easier while also allowing them to have some control over it.

Embracing Selective Attention

Barry Schwartz argues in *The Paradox of Choice* that contrary to popular belief, eliminating choices reduces decision making anxieties and improves happiness. Indeed, humans are born with selective attention. We tend to channel our attention toward relevant stimuli and block out irrelevant ones. It allows us to filter and process information with our limited attention span and focus on what is important.

Too many product choices, commercial messages, and channel options distract us from making what should be a simple buying decision. We have come to expect that complex decision making should never be our job and that companies are responsible for simplifying the options and making the best recommendation. AI technology should replace selective attention filtering in our minds so it is more manageable to make decisions in the era of information overload.

With millions of customer profiles and reviews, companies should be able to match specific customer needs with solutions. In consumer-packaged goods, for example, AI algorithms should be able to suggest the exact product variant and decide from which distribution center to send it. In the insurance sector, AI models may empower companies to set an optimized coverage bundle and pricing based on the past behavior of policyholders.

Allowing Individual Control

Rooted in human nature is the desire to have control over oneself and the environment. Having a perceived control—the sense of being in charge of our decisions and the outcomes—is shown to improve happiness. Thus, businesses should demonstrate that technology facilitates customers to have this sort of control over their buying decisions.

Limiting the choices for customers does not mean providing them with only one given option. Customers should still be able to make the customization on top of the automated personalization made by companies. Every customer desires a different level of control over product choice and touchpoint selection. Technology allows companies to predict their desire for control and provide the right balance between personalization and customization.

It should be a co-creation process between companies and customers not only in product selection but also in the overall customer experience. Every customer will want to have unique sets of experiences when interacting with the same products or services. Making products and touchpoints unbundled and modular allows customers to pick and choose the customer experience component they want. It is essentially a co-creation of experiences, which in turn will increase the sense of ownership from the customer side.

Technology Can Be Social

Social media have changed customer attitudes and expectations toward businesses. Most customers believe their social networks are more than advertising and expert opinions. Buying decisions are now driven not only by individual preference but also by a desire for social conformity. Social media also raise expectations. Customers require access to social customer care and demand instant responses. Humans are social, but social media have taken our social tendencies a step further.

In Marketing 5.0, companies need to respond to this by adopting social technologies in their customer-facing and back-end processes. The most popular frontline application is for social customer care, providing an alternative communication channel for customer interaction. For internal use, companies may adopt social tools to facilitate employee communications, enable knowledge sharing, and foster collaboration.

Technologies are more desirable when they enable and promote social connections. Creating social media channels is a start, but it should not stop there. AI allows companies to dive into and make sense of these social connection data. This deep learning uncovers insights on how to craft the right message and influence behaviors of the people in social networks.

Facilitating Interpersonal Connection

As humans, we are born vulnerable and dependent on our parents and caretakers to fulfill our basic needs. Gradually during childhood, we learn to communicate and interact with those around us as a primary method of intellectual and emotional learning. When interacting, we exchange ideas and stories as well as mirror our expressions and emotions with our counterparts.

That is why human brains are wired to be social very early in our lives.

Our nature as social beings explains the success of social media as a technological application. We like to listen to other people's personal experiences and express our own. As an exchange of visual cues, social media create an alternative platform to fulfill our social needs beyond face-to-face conversations.

Other applications of technology in business should also leverage the human desire for a social connection. Technology may facilitate the sharing of experiences and information, for instance, through blogs, forums, and wikis. Conversations should be expanded, not only between companies and customers but also between customers themselves. The crowdsourcing model is an example of how technology connects people with different competencies and skills to collaborate. Furthermore, technology-powered social commerce facilitates trade between buyers and sellers in a digital marketplace.

Driving the Pursuit of Aspiration

As social beings, we observe other people's life stories and relate them to ours. Friends in our social networks become our benchmarks. We aim to emulate the behavior and lifestyle of others, especially those with seemingly more exciting lives—driven by fear of missing out (FOMO). Personal expectations are now set by social environments that continually influence and motivate us to achieve bigger goals.

Technology should tap into this hidden pursuit of aspiration embedded in social networks. AI-powered content marketing, gamification, and social media may support humans' innate desire for peer recognition and social climb. Instead of patronizing customers with suggestions and recommendations, AI should exercise influence subtly through existing role models—friends, family, and community—which they listen to more than companies.

When leveraging social influence, however, businesses should go beyond selling products and services. Technology may become a powerful behavioral modification tool that drives digital activism and ultimately social change. Inspiring and encouraging people to pursue a more responsible lifestyle through social networks may become a significant contribution of technology to humanity.

Technology Can Be Experiential

Customers evaluate companies not only from the quality of products and services. They rate the overall customer journey, which encompasses all touchpoints across all channels. Therefore, innovation should focus not only on products but also on the whole experience. Aside from establishing product differentiation, companies should intensify communications, strengthen channel presence, and improve customer service.

The rise of digitalization drives the demand for an omnichannel experience. Customers continuously move from one channel to another—from online to offline and vice versa—and expect a seamless and consistent experience without a noticeable disconnect. Businesses must provide integrated high-tech and high-touch interactions.

In Marketing 5.0, back-end technologies such as AI and blockchain play a significant role in powering the seamless integration. On the other hand, front-end technologies such as sensors, robotics, voice command, as well as augmented and virtual reality may enhance the in-person touchpoints across the customer journey.

Empowering High-Touch Interaction

One of the weaknesses of a machine is its inability to replicate human touch. Advanced robotics and artificial skins with sensors are already in development to address this challenge.

But it is not only about recreating realistic feel but also about interpreting various and complex emotions from a simple human touch.

Humans can decode the emotions of their counterparts merely by touch. Research by Matthew Hertenstein revealed that we are capable—with an accuracy of up to 78%—of communicating to others, via touch, eight different emotions: anger, fear, disgust, sadness, sympathy, gratitude, love, and happiness. It is complicated to teach these subjective emotions to machines that only rely on logical, consistent, and quantifiable patterns.

Thus, the delivery of products and services may still require balancing between high-tech and high-touch interactions. Technology, however, can play an important role in delivering the high touch. The low-value clerical work should be taken over by a machine—allowing frontline staff to focus and spend more time on customer-facing activities. The effectiveness of in-person touchpoints can also be enhanced by AI-assisted customer profiling, providing clues for frontline staff to adjust their communication approach and offer the right solution.

Providing Constant Engagement

Humans tend to have a stable happiness level. When having an exciting and positive experience, happiness may temporarily increase, but it will eventually come back to the baseline level. Similarly, when having a discouraging and negative experience, happiness may drop, but it will bounce back to the original level. In psychology, it is called the hedonic treadmill—a term coined by Brickman and Campbell—in which satisfaction toward life experience always gravitates toward a certain baseline.

That is the reason why, as customers, we are easily bored and never feel truly satisfied. We want constant engagement throughout the customer journey. And from time to time, companies must refine and renew their customer experience to prevent us from switching to competitors.

To continually create a novel customer experience is a challenging feat. But with digitalization, companies can speed up the time to market for customer experience innovation. It is easier for companies to perform rapid experimentation, concept testing, and prototyping in the digital space.

Digital customer experience innovation, however, has moved away from merely changing user interface design. From chatbot to virtual reality to voice control, emerging technologies are transforming how companies communicate with customers. Technologies such as AI, the IoT, and blockchain are also improving the back-end efficiency and therefore enabling a faster customer experience.

Summary: Making Tech Personal, Social, and Experiential

The digital divide still exists. It will take at least another ten years to reach universal Internet penetration. But access alone does not end the digital divide. To become a fully digital society, we need to apply technologies in all aspects of our lives, beyond merely online communications and social media. Despite fears and anxieties brought forth by digitalization, the benefits for humanity are apparent.

In Marketing 5.0, businesses need to demonstrate to the customers that the correct applications of technology may improve human happiness. Technology enables a personalized approach to solving their problems while still allowing optional customization. Customers must be convinced that digitalization does not kill social relationships. Instead, it provides a platform to build a more intimate connection between customers and their communities. The human–machine dichotomy needs to end. To deliver superior customer experience, the integration of high-tech and high-touch interactions is imperative (see Figure 4.2).

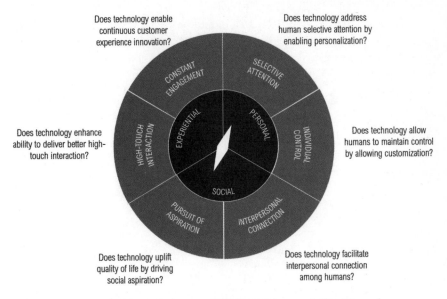

FIGURE 4.2   Technology Compass: Making It Personal, Social, and Experiential

REFLECTION QUESTIONS

- What are your personal views on technology? Think about how technology can empower or disrupt your organization.
- Assess if the technologies currently implemented in your organization enable you to provide personal, social, and experiential solutions to your customers.

PART III

New Strategies for Tech-Empowered Marketing

CHAPTER 5

The Digital-Ready Organization

One Strategy Doesn't Fit All

In the 1950s, a group of scientists experimented on monkeys on Kojima island. The scientists regularly dropped sweet potatoes on the beach sand for the monkeys to eat. One day, a young monkey named Imo learned that the potatoes would taste better if she washed them first. Imo began teaching her close friends and older family members about the new food hygiene habit. The change started slowly. But finally, when the majority of monkeys adopted the practice, the rest began to accept it as the new norm. The phenomenon is known as the hundredth-monkey effect, which refers to the required critical mass for a behavioral change to happen.

Similarly, younger generations are the ones leading the way when it comes to digital transformation. Generation Y and Generation Z combined are the biggest consumer market in history. Businesses are aligning their strategies to the preferences of these generations. And they are also the biggest in the workforce and are influencing companies from within. Thus, they have a tremendous impact on bringing digital technologies into the mainstream. But for the digital lifestyle to be the new norm, the change must be massive and evenly spread across generations and social-economic status.

The digitalization process happens fairly quickly around the world. On the one hand, everyone seems to embrace the digital lifestyle and cannot imagine living without it. And yet, the inertia still exists. Many customers are still accustomed to the traditional ways of buying and enjoying products and services. Equally, businesses have been procrastinating when it comes to digital transformation—the prerequisite for Marketing 5.0. The COVID-19 pandemic, however, has changed all that and opened everyone's mind on the need to go digital.

Case Study: COVID-19 as the Digitalization Accelerator

Global businesses have taken a hit due to the COVID-19 outbreak. Most companies are not ready as they have never faced such a pandemic. Every company seems to struggle with revenue decline and cash flow problems, all while managing employees who are personally hit by the outbreak. Companies may find themselves in the middle of confusion and dilemma to determine the right contingency plan to survive and even come back stronger.

The pandemic—and the social distancing it triggers—has pressed businesses to become more digital faster. During lockdowns and mobility restrictions around the world, customers were becoming more dependent on online platforms for their daily activities. We believe that it has changed the behavior not only during the crisis but for long after.

As customers were forced to stay at home for several months, they indeed became accustomed to the new digital lifestyle. They relied on e-commerce and food delivery apps to buy daily needs. Digital banking and cashless payment rose in volume. People were meeting others online through videoconferencing platforms such as Zoom and Google Meet. Children learned through online platforms at home while their parents worked from home. To kill time, people streamed more videos on YouTube and Netflix. And since health became of utmost importance, people connected with personal trainers or doctors remotely (see Figure 5.1).

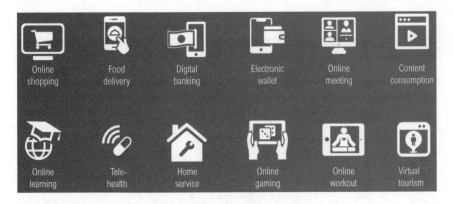

FIGURE 5.1 Digitalization Amid COVID-19

Businesses would never be the same again. Industries that used to rely heavily on physical interactions were forced to rethink their strategies. The food services industry adapted to the pandemic by boosting food delivery to compensate for the loss in dine-in revenue. Some restaurants switched to the cloud or ghost kitchens, serving only delivery orders. The travel industries turned to robot cleaners to sanitize rooms and trains. Airports, such as in the one in Bangalore, introduced "parking-to-boarding" contactless experiences.

As public transit ridership plummeted, transit authorities launched the micro-transit services. The on-demand buses and shuttles allowed passengers to order rides via mobile apps. Passengers could track not only the locations of buses but also the current capacity. It is useful to ensure physical tools and enable contact tracing. Automakers and dealers invested heavily in online sales platforms to serve the growing demand for digital interactions. Above all, every brand across different industries raised its digital content marketing game, aiming to engage customers via social media.

Companies could no longer procrastinate on digitalization when their sustainability depended on it. The crisis indeed exposed the readiness—or rather the unreadiness—of specific market segments and industry players to go digital.

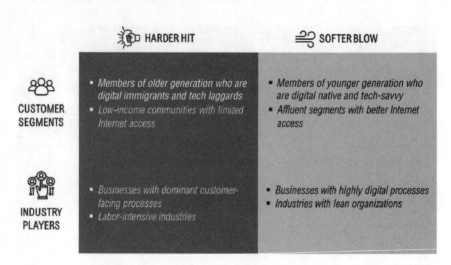

FIGURE 5.2   How COVID-19 Has Affected Different Customer Segments and Industry Players

Particular demographics known to be digital immigrants and laggards will be the hardest-hit segments as social distancing significantly alters their face-to-face routines. On the other hand, digital natives might thrive under these same conditions.

Likewise, the outbreak seems to cause more significant problems for some industries, although no business is immune to its effect. The sectors that require more direct physical interactions and are labor-intensive might suffer more. On the other hand, industries with highly digital business processes and lean organizations might be in a much better position (see Figure 5.2).

Digital Readiness Assessment

The different degree of readiness dictates the digitalization strategy to pursue. Thus, it is essential to establish a diagnostic tool for readiness assessment. The assessment must take into account both the supply and demand sides. The first step is to determine if the market—the demand side—is ready and willing to migrate to more digital touchpoints. The next step—from the supply side—is to evaluate the ability of companies to digitalize their business processes to take advantage of the migration. The two considerations make up a matrix that maps a company's position in the digital readiness quadrants.

To illustrate the four categories in the framework, we assess the digital readiness of six industry sectors: high-tech, financial services, grocery retailing, automotive, hospitality, and healthcare. The position of each sector is based on the current situation in the United States, and it may change over time as the market evolves. Customers in other markets may have different degrees of readiness. The readiness of industry players in each industry may also vary (see Figure 5.3).

#1 "Origin" Quadrant

This quadrant includes industries that are the hardest hit during the pandemic. Companies in these industries would be less

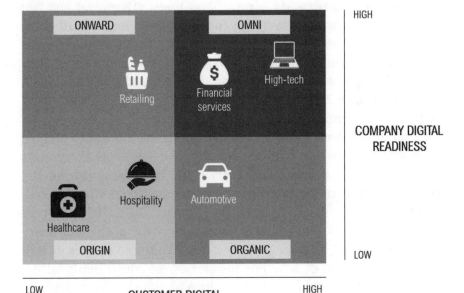

FIGURE 5.3   Digital Readiness by Industry

ready to face this crisis mainly because their business processes still include significant physical interactions, which are harder to eliminate or substitute for. At the same time, it is also unlikely for them to migrate customers to digital touchpoints, mostly due to the lack of urgency for purchase during a crisis. The examples in this quadrant are the hospitality and healthcare industries, which rely heavily on human-to-human interactions. For players in these industries, it is a chicken-and-egg dilemma: invest in digitalization or wait for customers to migrate to digital behavior.

The hospitality industry has been disrupted by digitalization for many years. The travel review sites and online booking platforms have brought transparency to service quality and pricing. Online lodging marketplaces such as Airbnb have also put pressure on large hotel chains. But the digitalization mostly occurs in front and back segments of the customer journey. Customers use digital tools to plan and book trips as well as to review and recommend destinations. But the middle section of the customer journey is largely nondigital.

And the digitalization is mostly on the surface level and not yet at a transformative level for the industry. The form of technology used is only basic, leveraging the Internet mainly for digital ads, content marketing, and electronic channels. A few hospitality players have made sporadic attempts to use advanced technologies such as robotics and the Internet of Things (IoT), but customer responses have been lukewarm.

The healthcare industry has somewhat the same degree of digital readiness. Artificial intelligence (AI) has the power to transform healthcare, and early signs have been promising. Despite the potential, healthcare delivery is still very traditional, involving face-to-face interactions. Before the COVID-19 outbreak, telehealth was not really an option for both healthcare providers and their patients. After the pandemic is over, it will remain a question of whether the trend will continue its stride. Aside from the regulatory barrier, providers seem to struggle to provide the infrastructure and healthcare professionals who are digital-ready. And it is doubtful whether the payers will have the same willingness to pay for telehealth.

#2 "Onward" Quadrant

The next quadrant consists of industries and companies that have difficulty migrating customers despite having invested in significant digitalization of their business processes. Industry sectors in this quadrant have digital ecosystems in place and have been incentivizing customers to go digital for some time. But most customers are still stuck in inertia and digital adoption has been limited.

One example is the retailing industry. As a digital native, Amazon has dominated the e-commerce scene for many years. It even stepped up its grocery retailing operations by acquiring Whole Foods. On the other hand, long before the pandemic, brick-and-mortar retailers had also started the digital transformation in anticipation of incoming disruption. Retailing giant Walmart launched Walmart.com for e-commerce and partnered with Shopify to expand its marketplace operations. The moves allow the two big retailers to go head-to-head in providing an omnichannel experience.

The supporting infrastructure is also growing, enabling e-commerce to expand. Although some big retailers build their logistic capabilities, companies like DHL invest in an e-commerce fulfillment network. Social media also make a foray into the online shopping sphere by providing the social selling platform. Target, for instance, has become the first big retailer to sell products via Instagram.

Despite the highly established ecosystems, the Census Bureau reported that in the first quarter of 2020, e-commerce only contributed to slightly less than 12% of the total retail trade. Pew also reveals that although 80% of Americans shop online, most of them still prefer to go to the stores. But the pandemic could create a new normal where the bulk of shoppers migrate to a more digital customer journey. Industry players need to monitor the trend closely to see if the pandemic is a big enough catalyst for online retailing.

#3 "Organic" Quadrant

This quadrant applies to industries that deliver products and services with a high degree of physical touchpoints. Most of the time, these industries are also labor-intensive and thus have difficulty managing their employees remotely. On the other hand, most of the customers are ready to migrate to go digital. They will become primary drivers, forcing companies to adopt digital technologies.

The automotive industry is one of the sectors in this quadrant. Most car buyers are already webrooming. That is, they conduct research online and eventually buy at the dealers. Google/comScore research shows that 95% of car buyers use digital as the primary source of information, but more than 95% of purchases still happen at the dealership.

But the pandemic has accelerated online car buying. Several car-buying platforms such as Carvana and Vroom have reported a surge in online car buying as buyers prefer contactless interaction. Unlike in the hospitality and healthcare sectors, physical contacts in car buying are unnecessary and less valuable once potential buyers have done considerable research.

Moreover, cars have increasingly become high-tech products with the electric vehicle (EV), autonomous vehicle (AV), and vehicle-to-vehicle (V2V) connectivity trends on the horizon. As car usage experience becomes increasingly high-tech, the buying process is the only major step in the customer journey still traditional.

Yet, the automakers and dealers have just started to build digital capabilities. Aside from online car buying platforms, most automakers and dealers have limited online presence. Customer expectations toward the automotive industry digitalization are not only restricted to an e-commerce platform for online test-drive reservations and purchase but also the adoption of other digital sales and marketing tools. With virtual reality (VR), for example, potential buyers can explore car options visually. More importantly, AI can provide additional features such as predictive vehicle maintenance and preventive safety monitoring by utilizing connected car data.

#4 "Omni" Quadrant

This quadrant is ultimately where the companies want to be. Businesses in other quadrants should try to migrate their customers and build their capabilities to become an Omni company. The Omni quadrant belongs to industries that are experiencing a softer blow during the COVID-19 crisis, with high-tech and financial services as two industry examples. Tech companies are naturally the readiest for social distancing policy and stay-at-home behavior. With digitalization as a major part of their DNA, the companies have aimed to disrupt traditional industries, and the pandemic simply gave them a significant push. Companies like Amazon, Microsoft, Netflix, Zoom, and Salesforce have all experienced high growth.

Digital financial services also grow when customers avoid trips to the banks, and cashless payments have become the norm. Banks, however, have been migrating their customers to digital channels with all sorts of incentives long before the outbreak. Today, all big banks offer online and mobile banking facilities.

In banking, the customer's choice of channel is purely based on convenience. Customers who choose to go to a bank branch do not look for a touchy-feely experience like in the brick-and-mortar stores. They want to go to the branch because it is more convenient. Thus, if digital banking can replicate convenience for a wide range of customers, the electronic channel will become the most preferred.

But the digitalization goes far deeper than that in the industry. Financial services have been exploring the use of chatbots for reducing the call center workload, blockchain for enhancing transaction security, and AI to detect fraud. It has become one of the most digital industries aside from the high-tech and media businesses.

How Ready Are You to Go Digital?

The four quadrants give a general view of how prepared a particular industry is to go digital. But every company, even in the same industry sector, might have different readiness and therefore find itself in a different quadrant from its peers. Thus, each company may perform a self-assessment based on its ability to go digital and the desire of its customers to migrate to digital channels. Businesses that fit most criteria in the assessment are ready for digitalization (see Figure 5.4).

COMPANY DIGITAL READINESS

	Digital customer experience
1	The company can engage with customers digitally to a large extent across customer journeys.
2	All the digital touchpoints can be integrated into a seamless and frictionless customer experience.
3	The company can create value and capture revenue through digital business models.
	Digital infrastructure
1	Technologies to capture, store, manage, analyze a large volume of customer data in real-time are available.
2	Business processes are digitalized and re-engineered to fit the new digital business model.
3	The digitalization of physical assets, such as buildings, fleet, and equipment with IoT, is implemented.
	Digital organization
1	Most employees are empowered with digital tools to work remotely and collaborate with others virtually.
2	Building digital talents, such as data scientists, UX designers, and IT architect, is a key priority.
3	Strong digital culture exists, enabling alignment between business managers and digital talents.

CUSTOMER DIGITAL READINESS

	Digital customer base
1	Majority of the customer base are Generation Y and Generation Z who are digital savvy.
2	Most customers already engage and transact with the company via digital platforms.
3	When consuming or using the products and services, customers are required to interact with digital interfaces.
	Digital customer journey
1	The customer journeys are already entirely or partially online (webrooming or showrooming).
2	Physical touchpoints that customers find frustrating can be replaced and enhanced by digital technologies.
3	A wealth of information is available on the Internet for customers to make well-informed decisions by themselves.
	Customer propensity to go digital
1	Customers deem physical interactions with the company to be unnecessary, irrelevant, and of no value.
2	The products and services are considered less complicated, and thus the risks and trust issues are limited.
3	Most customers have more incentives to go digital: more choices, better prices, higher quality, better convenience.

FIGURE 5.4 Digital Readiness Assessment

Strategies to Migrate Customers to Digital Channels

Companies in the Origin and Onward quadrants need to migrate customers to digital channels. Their customers still see value in physical interactions, thus have low motivation to go digital. The migration strategy should focus on providing the stimulus for going digital while delivering higher value via online customer experience.

#1 Provide the Incentive to Go Digital

To promote digital interactions, companies must show the benefits of going online. They may provide positive and negative incentives to encourage digital migration. Positive incentives may take the form of instant gratification, such as cashback, discounts, and consumer promotions on digital platforms. Negative incentives may take the form of additional charges upon selecting an offline method during interactions, or in extreme cases, companies can make the offline mode unavailable to access.

Aside from monetary incentives, a company can inform customers about its digital capabilities and how it would improve the way to do business.

#2 Address Frustration Points with Digital

Companies need to identify customer frustration points across the customer journey and address them with digitalization. Physical interactions have inherent weaknesses, particularly regarding their inefficiencies. A leading cause of frustration is a long wait time or queue in offline touchpoints. Complicated processes also often lead to confusion and a waste of customers' time. For customers who want quick and straightforward resolutions, digital can take over some of the processes.

Moreover, human interactions have high risks of service failure. Incompetent staff, unstandardized responses, and poor hospitality are some of the leading causes of complaints. When the frontline problems are getting more apparent, especially as businesses scale up, making an alternative digital channel available might stimulate behavior change.

#3 Recreate Desired Physical Interactions with Digital

When human-to-human interactions create value and are still desirable, businesses can utilize digitally enabled communications. Customers can connect with frontline staff, who can work from anywhere, via a video platform. Examples include video banking in financial services and virtual consultation in telehealth. The approach saves costs while still preserving the benefits of human touchpoints.

A more advanced approach is to use a chatbot that can replace the frontline staff for basic inquiries and consultations. Virtual assistants with voice tech are now capable of answering simple questions and executing commands. Despite some limitations, natural language processing (NLP) technology enables conversations to be natural.

Strategies to Build Digital Capabilities

The challenge for businesses in the Origin and Organic quadrants is to build capabilities that address the needs of digital customers. The companies need to invest in digital infrastructure— hardware, software, and IT systems—that will be the foundation to deliver digital customer experience. Ultimately, they must build organization capabilities, which include digital expertise, skills, and agile culture.

#1 Invest in Digital Infrastructure

Companies need to start their digital investment by building customer data infrastructure. Digitalization unlocks many new tactics, such as one-to-one personalization and predictive marketing. But the foundation for those tactics is the rapid and dynamic understanding of customers. Thus, companies need technologies to manage and analyze big data in real time.

Companies must also transform their business processes. Digitalization is not merely automation of current operations. Companies often have to reengineer the entire business to fit with the new digital reality. Moreover, digital immigrant companies have amassed physical assets that need to be digitalized. With the Internet of Things that connects those assets digitally, the value of the assets can go up. Companies can utilize smart buildings or smart fleets to deliver a real omnichannel experience.

#2 Develop Digital Customer Experience

In the post-pandemic era, businesses that manage to build digital customer experience will flourish. The digitalization should not stop at basic customer engagement. Instead, it must be all-encompassing across customer touchpoints from marketing to sales, distribution, product delivery, and service. And all those digital touchpoints must be orchestrated into a synchronized customer experience.

But most importantly, they need to rethink their ways of creating value, or in other words, how to generate revenue from the customer experience. Digital businesses have entirely different sets of economics. Companies must consider emerging business models such as everything-as-a-service subscription, electronic marketplace, or on-demand models.

#3 Establish Strong Digital Organization

Perhaps the most crucial factor that determines the success of the digital transformation is the organization. Employees must be empowered with digital tools to work remotely and collaborate with others virtually. In traditional companies in the process of transforming, these new digital tools need to integrate with the legacy IT systems.

To accelerate the organizational learning process, companies need to recruit new digital talents such as data scientists, UX designers, and IT architects. Companies must also focus on the culture, which is often the main barrier to digital transformations. What they need to build is an agile culture with rapid experimentation as well as continuous collaboration between business managers and digital talents.

Strategies to Strengthen Digital Leadership

In the face of increased customer expectations, companies in the Omni quadrant must not stand still. With others catching up, these companies are under pressure to raise the bar. Digital customers—Generation Y and Generation Z—are no longer satisfied with the basics. Companies must adopt advanced technologies ("the next tech") into the customer experience ("the new CX").

#1 Adopt the Next Tech

For Omni companies, content marketing on social media and e-commerce platforms are considered hygiene factors without which they cannot compete. To step up their game, companies need to adopt more advanced technologies that are not yet mainstream. They must consider using AI to power up their marketing activities. An example is the use of natural language processing technology to empower chatbots and voice assistants.

A combination of AI, biometrics, sensors, and IoT can help companies to deliver a digitally powered physical touchpoint that is both personalized to each individual and contextual to the exact moment of interaction. The use of augmented reality and virtual reality can spice up the marketing campaign and product exploration. These technologies can be game-changers, and it is the responsibility of the digital leaders to be the pioneers. (For more detailed discussions on the next tech, see Chapter 6.)

#2 Introduce the New CX

A frictionless journey is the dream of every customer. The switch from offline to online and vice versa used to be very painful since the touchpoints were disjointed and worked in silos. Customers were not recognized instantly and had to introduce themselves every time they moved between channels. With digitalization, the frictionless customer experience—in which the whole value is greater than the sum of its parts—can finally be a reality. This is the new CX.

Companies must focus on delivering the new CX at three different levels: informative, interactive, and immersive. Whenever customers seek for answers, long for conversations, and surround themselves with sensory experiences, companies should be ready to deliver. (More information on the new CX can be found in Chapter 7.)

#3 Strengthen Position as the Digital-First Brand

Being a digital-first brand means putting all the resources to serve the needs of digital customers before addressing the rest. It is not about being a high-tech company or having the best IT infrastructure. It is about having the overall vision and strategy that puts everything digital at the core. CX design should center around bridging between the physical and the digital world. Building digital assets becomes the number-one priority. Digital products are first in the pipeline. And most importantly, every person and every process in the organization is digital-ready (see Figure 5.5).

COVID-19 has helped customers distinguish the real digital-first brands from the wannabes. The sudden impact of the pandemic has left companies unprepared. The digital-first brands thrive during the crisis without exerting extra effort.

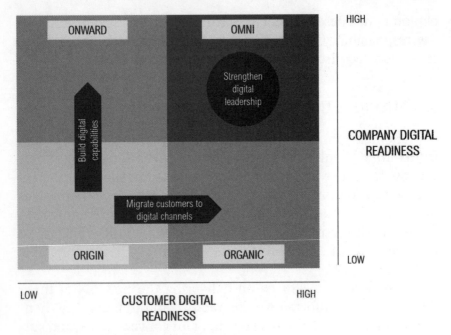

FIGURE 5.5   The Digitalization Strategies

Summary: One Size Doesn't Fit All

The COVID-19 pandemic has unexpectedly become a digital accelerator globally. Businesses and markets alike were forced to adapt to restricted mobility and hence relied heavily on digital. It has become a wake-up call for companies to stop procrastinating in their digitalization efforts. A digital-ready organization is prepared for what comes next as digital natives take over the markets all around the world.

But when it comes to digitalization, there is no one-size-fits-all approach. Every industry sector and every player in the industry will be in a different state of digital maturity. The first step is to assess the digital readiness of the customer base in which they are competing. The next is to self-evaluate the digital capabilities of the organization. Depending on the readiness assessment, companies will need to craft and execute different strategies, which may include customer migration as well as digital transformation strategies.

REFLECTION QUESTIONS

- Assess the digital readiness of your organization as well as that of your customers. How ready are you to go digital?
- Think about how you can improve your organization's digital readiness and create a plan to implement the transformation.

CHAPTER 6

The Next Tech

It's Time for Human-Like Technologies to Take Off

During World War II, the Germans extensively used the Enigma machine to encrypt military communications. Intercepting and breaking the encrypted codes would allow the British and the Allies to anticipate the movement of German forces. To prevent more war casualties, a group of scientists raced against time to decipher the military codes by creating a machine called the Bombe. After several attempts to "train" the Bombe, they finally succeeded. One of the scientists was Alan Turing, a mathematician widely credited as one of the very first thinkers in artificial intelligence (AI). His personal goal was to create a machine that could learn from experience—paving the way for machine learning.

Similar to how the early form of AI helped the Allies win World War II, technologies will empower businesses and allow companies to do things that were not possible before. The next tech—those technologies that will be mainstream in the next decade—will be the foundation of Marketing 5.0. It liberates companies from past business limitations. Tedious, repetitive tasks that typically cause human errors can be automated. Tele-technologies can help companies overcome geographical hurdles. The use of blockchain enhances security in data-sensitive industries, such as financial services. The use of robotics and the Internet of Things (IoT) reduces the need for human resources in high-risk environments.

But most importantly, the next tech allows for a more human-istic marketing approach. Augmented and virtual reality—or mixed reality (MR)—allow companies to visualize their offering to customers, for example, in the real estate sector. Sensors and artificial intelligence enable companies to personalize their content, such as in facial recognition–powered advertising billboards.

Next Tech Made Possible

It is important to note that much of the next tech was invented more than half a century ago. Artificial intelligence, natural language processing (NLP), and programmable robotics, for instance, have all been around since the 1950s. The initial work on facial recognition started in the 1960s. But why are they on the rise only in recent years? The answer lies in the enabling technologies that were not as powerful as they are today. Computers were not as powerful, and data storage was still bulky and expensive. The rise of the next tech is indeed made possible by the maturity of six enablers: computing power, open-source software, the Internet, cloud computing, mobile devices, and big data (see Figure 6.1).

Computing Power

As technology becomes more advanced, it demands more powerful yet cost-efficient hardware. The exponential increase in **computing power**, especially the highly efficient graphics processing unit (GPU), has made it possible to operate power-hungry technology such as artificial intelligence. Advances in semiconductor technology and the shrinking size of processors means more power and lower energy consumption. It enables the AI machine to be small and local to empower applications

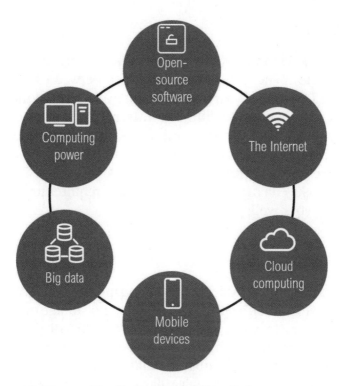

FIGURE 6.1 The Six Enablers of Next Tech

that need a real-time response, such as in an autonomous car or a robot.

Open-Source Software

An equally robust software system is needed to run the powerful hardware. It usually involved years of development in creating software for AI. Here is where **open-source software** plays a significant role in accelerating the process. Embracing collaboration, large companies such as Microsoft, Google, Facebook, Amazon, and IBM have been open-sourcing their AI research and algorithms. It leads to faster improvement and enhancement of the systems by the worldwide communities of developers. Similar open-source models apply in robotics, blockchain, and IoT.

The Internet

The most game-changing technology ever invented is probably **the Internet**. The network convergence between fiber to the home (FTTH) and 5G wireless technology fulfills the increasing need for Internet bandwidth. The Internet connects billions of not only people but also machines. It is also the foundation for networking-related technologies such as IoT and blockchain. Interactive technologies such as AR, VR, and voice assistant also rely immensely on high-speed Internet as it requires low network latency to work well.

Cloud Computing

Another important enabler is **cloud computing**—shared access to computer systems, especially software and storage on the web, allowing users to work remotely. The COVID-19 pandemic— and the remote work it imposes—make cloud computing more critical to businesses. Companies that use cloud computing do not need to invest in expensive hardware and software to run complex applications such as AI. Instead, they typically subscribe to services and use shared infrastructure offered by cloud computing providers. It gives companies the flexibility to scale the subscription as their needs grow. And as providers regularly update their infrastructure, companies do not need to worry about keeping up with the latest technology. Five big players in AI also dominate the cloud computing market: Amazon, Microsoft, Google, Alibaba, and IBM.

Mobile Devices

The trend of distributed computing is made possible by the development of **mobile devices**. Mobile computing development has been so tremendous that high-end smartphones are now as powerful as a PC, making it the primary computing and Internet access device for most people. The portability of the devices empowers mobility and in turn increases productivity on-the-go.

It also allows the distributed delivery of customer experiences. Today, smartphones are robust enough to power facial recognition, voice assistant, AR, VR, and even 3D printing.

Big Data

Big data serves as the final piece of the puzzle. AI technology requires a massive volume and a wide variety of data to train the machine and improve the algorithm from time to time. The daily use of web browsers, email, social media, and messaging applications, especially on mobile devices, provides that. The external data supplement the internal transaction data by providing psychographic and behavioral patterns. What is great about Internet-based data is that unlike traditional market research data, they can be gathered online, in real time, and at scale. Moreover, the cost of data storage is falling, and the capacity is increasing at a faster pace—making it easy to manage the large volume of information.

The availability as well as the affordability of the six interrelated technologies encourage academic and corporate labs to explore the next frontier. It makes previously dormant advanced technologies able to reach maturity and large-scale adoption.

Reimagining Business with the Next Tech

Humans are unique beings, blessed with unparalleled cognitive ability. We are capable of making tough decisions and solving complex problems. But most importantly, we can learn from experience. The way our brain develops cognitive skills is through contextual learning: acquiring knowledge, finding relevance based on our own life experience, and developing our holistic views.

The way humans learn is also extraordinarily complex. Humans receive stimuli from all five senses. We use verbal language and visual cues to teach and learn. Our perceptions of the world are enhanced by touch, smell, and taste. We also receive psychomotor training, for example, to be able to write, walk, and perform other motor skills. This entire learning is a lifetime process. As a result, humans can communicate, sense, and move based on environmental stimuli.

For many years, scientists and technologists have been obsessed with replicating human capabilities with machines. Machine learning in AI attempts to mimic the contextual learning approach. AI engines are not designed to learn on their own. Like humans, they must be trained on what to learn using algorithms. They find relevance from big data that serve as contextual examples. Finally, they can "comprehend" the algorithms and make complete sense of the data.

Sensors play a role in helping the learning by mimicking human senses. For example, facial and image recognition can help machines distinguish objects based on the visual learning model that humans use. Furthermore, the cognitive skill of computers allows them to mimic social communications—with NLP—and make physical movements—with robotics. Although machines are yet to possess human-level consciousness and finesse, they have better endurance and reliability, making it possible to learn a massive volume of knowledge in a short period.

Human uniqueness, however, does not stop there. Humans can comprehend abstract concepts, such as ethics, cultures, and love, that have no physical forms. This imagination capability beyond reasoning makes humans more creative. And it sometimes drives humans to deviate from what is considered rational and reasonable. Moreover, humans are highly social. We intuitively like to gather in groups and build relationships with others.

Machines are also being trained with these other aspects of human capabilities. For example, AR and VR try to mimic human imagination by overlaying two different realities—online and offline—on top of each other. We also try to conceptualize how machines should "socialize" with one another by developing IoT and blockchain.

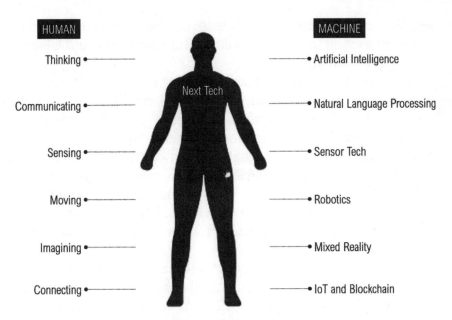

FIGURE 6.2   Bionics: Six Ways Technology Mimics Humans

We call these advanced technologies the next tech: artificial intelligence, NLP, sensor tech, robotics, mixed reality, IoT, and blockchain. By replicating human capabilities, they will empower the next-generation marketing (see Figure 6.2).

Artificial Intelligence

AI is probably the most popular, yet the least understood technology in recent times. It is intimidating when we think of it as human-level, as seen in science fiction movies. This form of AI is known as artificial general intelligence (AGI), which has human-level consciousness but is still in development for at least another 20 years.

But it does not need to be that sophisticated. Narrow applications of AI are already common, being used extensively to automate routine tasks in several industries. Financial services companies have been using it to automate fraud detection and credit scoring. With AI, Google has been recommending searches even as you type each letter on the search bar. Amazon has been using it to provide book recommendations, and Uber to set dynamic pricing.

In its narrow form, AI uses computer algorithms to perform specific tasks that once required human intelligence. The way the computer learns is either supervised or unsupervised. In supervised learning, human programmers map the algorithm in input–output or if–then format. An early form of this is known as the expert system, primarily found in customer service chatbots. When interacting with a simple chatbot, customers can only ask questions from a predetermined list. Companies that have recurring and standardized processes may utilize the expert system for automation.

In unsupervised AI, the computer learns and discovers previously unknown patterns as it feeds past historical data with minimum human involvement. The AI analyzes and transforms unstructured data into structured information. The applications in the marketing field are plenty. One of the most important is to interpret and draw insights from big data. From social media posts, transaction history, and other behavioral data, AI can group customers into clusters—enabling companies to perform data-driven market segmentation and targeting. It is a foundation that allows companies to provide customization and personalization in product recommendation, pricing, and content marketing campaigns. As customers respond to these offerings, the computer continues to learn and modify its algorithm.

Although AGI is not yet available, an integrated AI in a company is possible. Take Ant Financial, the parent company of online payment Alipay and an affiliate of Alibaba. The company utilizes AI and other supporting technologies to automate all its core business processes: payment security, financial advisory, loan approval, insurance claim processing, customer service, and risk management. It reimagines car insurance, for example, using image recognition and machine learning. Customers can submit a car insurance claim with a smartphone photo. The AI engine will analyze the image and determine if the request is legitimate.

AI is simply the brain of automation. It needs to work with other technologies such as robotics, facial recognition, voice tech, and sensors to deliver the next-generation customer experience. Previously in the domain of the computing research lab, AI has now reached far and wide into the everyday lives of customers. AI will create value but must be carefully managed. Biases, coming from human preferences and historical decisions, may sneak into the AI algorithm. And without inclusive development, AI may lead to a widening income disparity.

Natural Language Processing (NLP)

Another exciting development is in the area of NLP. It is about teaching machines to replicate the human way of communicating, which covers both written and spoken language. NLP is a critical aspect in the development of AI, especially for one requiring language inputs, such as in voice assistants. It is also a challenging feat since the human language, in its natural form, is often fuzzy, intricate, and layered. A large volume of real conversation transcripts and video recordings is required to teach machines the nuances of language.

The most widespread application of NLP is for chatbots. Chatbots are being utilized not only for servicing but also for selling. It will reduce the need for higher-cost channels such as inbound call centers and outbound telemarketing, especially when it comes to serving lower-tier customers. Companies like Lyft, Sephora, and Starbucks are already using chatbots for order taking and customer interactions. In B2B space, companies like HubSpot and RapidMiner use chatbots to qualify leads and direct prospects to the right follow-up channels. The popularity of online messaging platforms, such as WhatsApp, Facebook Messenger, and WeChat, is the key contributor to the rise of chatbots. For the same reason, people expect to communicate with chatbots in the same way they would chat with other people.

It is why NLP is so important. Unlike simple chatbots capable of answering only closed-ended questions, NLP-powered chatbots can interpret and respond to arbitrary questions. NLP allows chatbots to understand a chat message, although it contains noise such as typos, slang, and abbreviations. Powerful chatbots can also understand sentiments, for example, to detect sarcastic statements. And they are capable of understanding the context to infer the intended meaning of ambiguous words.

With voice tech, machines have also gotten much better at responding to verbal commands. There are many available voice assistants: Amazon Alexa, Apple Siri, Google Assistant, and Microsoft Cortana. These applications are already very capable of answering simple queries and executing commands in multiple languages. The Google I/O demo of the Duplex in 2018 demonstrated how a virtual assistant could also smoothly carry out natural conversations. When calling a salon or a restaurant to book an appointment, the voice assistant ditches the robotic tone and even adds the use of pauses and filler words, making it more realistic than ever.

With this recent development, more and more customers begin to search and shop via voice assistants. The assistants will compare products and make recommendations on brands to buy based on historical decisions—the more products purchased, the more accurate the suggestion. To anticipate this whole new way to shop, brands need to be ready and collect big data on their own to understand the purchase algorithms, which reflect the user preferences.

Sensor Tech

Aside from text and speech recognition, computers also learn from image and facial recognition. The growing popularity of photos and selfies in the era of social media fuels this trend. In a nutshell, what image recognition does is scan an image and look on the web or database for a resemblance. As a leading search engine, Google has developed image recognition capabilities whereby people can perform a search using an image.

The application for image recognition is immense. For example, browsing through millions of social media posts, companies can scan photos of people buying and consuming their brands and send thank-you notes. They can also identify people using competing brands and invite them to switch. This highly targeted advertising is a very efficient way to improve market share.

Tesco in the UK uses image recognition sensors extensively to improve their planograms, which show how retail products should be displayed on the shelves to encourage more purchases. It deploys robots to take photos of products on the shelves and analyze the images to identify stockouts and misplacements. The image recognition capability is also useful to improve customer experience. For instance, customers may scan a product on the shelf and receive detailed information about the product from an AI engine.

Tesco also plans to deploy a facial recognition camera on checkout counters to identify the age of alcohol and cigarette shoppers. It allows for self-checkout without the presence of a human cashier. Another use case of facial recognition software is for digital billboards. Identifying the demographic profile and emotional state of the audience can help advertisers deliver the right content. Capturing the facial responses to content also allows advertisers to improve their ads.

Another popular area of sensor deployment is in autonomous vehicles. Tech companies like Google-affiliated Waymo are competing with automaker-backed companies like GM Cruise, Ford Autonomous, and Argo AI in this area. A self-driving car heavily depends on sensors to feed the AI with an understanding of the surrounding condition. It typically uses four types of sensors—camera, radar, ultrasound, and lidar—situated in different parts of the vehicle to measure distance, identify road lanes, and detect other surrounding cars.

Telematics systems involving sensors are also installed in cars to improve safety and assist with vehicle management. It is particularly useful for logistics and supply chain optimization. Owners can monitor their driverless vehicles, receiving daily insights about GPS patterns, driving time, mileage, and fuel efficiency. More importantly, owners can get a reminder when their cars need servicing. Insurance companies like Progressive and GEICO also use telematics for usage-based insurance programs offering premium discounts.

Robotics

Since the 1960s, large companies in industrialized countries have primarily utilized robots for backend automation. Automation robots have shown the most cost-saving value in manufacturing due to its labor-intensive nature, especially in recent years when the costs of robots have fallen below the inflated wages. The advancement of AI has widened the range of tasks that industrial robots can handle. Combined with the endurance and work-hour flexibility of robots, which lead to better productivity, it makes a solid business case for companies to automate.

In recent years, companies have attempted to use robots to replace humans in customer-facing interfaces as a marketing exercise. Due to its aging population and tendency to accept a small number of immigrants, Japan is pushing forward and leading the way when it comes to robots. Japanese automakers like Toyota and Honda are investing in carebots for elderly assistance. Softbank's robot Pepper becomes a personal companion in nursing homes and a sales assistant in retail stores. Nestlé in Japan also uses robots to make, sell, and serve coffee.

But one of the most extreme experiments of robotics is perhaps in the hospitality sector, where the human role is crucial. The idea is that the robots will free up staff time to deliver a more personalized service. Hilton, in Virginia, piloted Connie, a robot concierge. Powered by IBM Watson AI, it can recommend nearby attractions and restaurants to hotel guests. Aloft Hotel in Cupertino introduced a robot butler called Botlr that delivers amenities and room service to hotel guests and receives tips in the form of tweets. Hotels are also beginning to use robots for cooking. Studio M Hotel in Singapore, for example, uses a robot chef to make an omelet.

Although we often visualize the humanoid form, robotics is not only about physical robots. A growing trend, robot process automation (RPA), involves software robotics. In RPA, the virtual robot performs computer work as a human would, following specific guidelines. Companies use it to automate high-volume, repetitive processes with no room for error. It is often used for back-office financial management, such as for invoicing and payment. Human resources management, such as employee onboarding and payroll processing, can also be automated.

In sales, RPA can be utilized in several ways. Managing CRM is one of the most common use cases. The sales team can easily convert business cards and aggregate paper reports to digital formats and store them in the CRM system. RPA is also useful to automate emails to sales leads. In marketing, RPA is mostly used for programmatic advertising—which involves automated bidding and buying of digital advertising placement for an optimized outcome. It is becoming more popular due to the increasing proportion of the online advertising budget.

Mixed Reality (MR)

In the field of three-dimensional user interface innovation, AR and VR—or mixed reality (MR)—stand out as one of the most promising, blurring the boundaries between physical and digital worlds. Since the objective is to emulate human imagination, current applications focus primarily on entertainment and gaming. But some brands have already invested in MR to enhance the customer experience.

In AR, interactive digital content overlays the user view of the real-world environments. Pokemon Go is a popular example of an AR-based mobile game, where imaginary creatures appear to be near our vicinity when seen through a mobile screen. The types of digital content to overlay have evolved over the years, from mainly visual graphics and sound to haptic feedback and olfactory sensation.

VR, in a way, is the reverse of AR. AR is like bringing digital objects to the real world, whereas VR is like bringing you to the digital world. VR typically replaces the user view with a simulated digital environment. With headsets on, users can experience riding in a rollercoaster or shooting aliens. To use VR, users can choose between dedicated headsets such as Oculus Rift or phone-based headsets like Google Cardboard. Game consoles from Sony and Nintendo also offer VR devices as extensions.

The ability to mix both the digital and the real world is a game-changer in marketing. It brings endless possibilities to deliver engaging content marketing, mainly since MR is rooted in video games. MR allows companies to embed additional information and stories into their products in a fun and exciting way. In turn, it will enable customers to visualize themselves not only seeing but using the products. In a way, customers are now able to "consume" the product even before deciding to buy it.

The tourism sector uses MR to offer a virtual tour to encourage people to visit the actual destination. The Louvre, for example, provides a virtual experience for users wearing HTC Vive VR headsets of not only seeing the *Mona Lisa* from close range but also to explore stories behind the painting. Retailers use it to try out the products virtually or to provide tutorials. IKEA, for example, produces 3D images of their products and uses AR to help potential buyers visualize how a piece of furniture fits in their homes. Lowe's uses VR to train users step-by-step on DIY home improvement.

In automotive, for example, AR is extensively used by Mercedes-Benz, Toyota, and Chevrolet in the form of a heads-up display that overlays information on the windshields. Land Rover extends the idea of the heads-up display by overlaying entire images of the terrain ahead onto the windshield, creating the illusion of a transparent car hood.

TOMS is an example of how VR is being used for marketing as well as creating social impact. The company is famous for its policy of donating one pair of shoes for every pair sold. With VR, TOMS allows customers to experience what it is like to give the shoes to the children in need.

Internet of Things (IoT) and Blockchain

IoT refers to the interconnectivity of machines and devices that communicate with one another. Mobile phones, wearables, home appliances, cars, smart electricity meters, and surveillance cameras are some examples of connected devices. Individuals can use IoT to power smart homes. Companies can use it for remote monitoring and tracking of assets such as building and fleet vehicles. But most importantly, IoT enables a seamless customer experience delivery. Frictionless experience is now possible since every physical touchpoint is digitally connected via IoT.

Disney serves as a case in point. The theme park leverages IoT to eliminate frictions and redefine its customer experience at the park. Integrated with My Disney Experience website, its MagicBand bracelet stores customer information and thus works as a theme park ticket, room key, and payment method. The band continually communicates with thousands of sensors in the rides, restaurants, stores, and hotels via a radio frequency technology. Disney staff can monitor customer movement, anticipate incoming guests within 40 feet, and proactively serve them. Imagine being greeted personally by your first name without needing to say anything. The collected data on guest movement is valuable to design location-based offerings or to recommend the most efficient park routes to a guest's favorite rides.

Blockchain is another form of distributed technology. An open and distributed ledger system, blockchain records encrypted data across a peer-to-peer network. A block is like a page of a ledger that contains all the past transactions. Once a block is completed, it can never be altered and will give way for the next block in the chain. The security of blockchain allows transactions between two parties without the bank as the middleman. It also allows the invention of bitcoin, a cryptocurrency, without needing a central bank.

The safe and transparent recordkeeping nature of blockchain is a potential game-changer for marketing. IBM, in collaboration with Unilever, embarked on a blockchain project to increase transparency in digital advertising placement. The Association of National Advertisers estimates that only 30 to 40 cents of every digital media dollar reaches publishers while the rest goes to the intermediaries. Blockchain is used to track this chain of transactions from the advertisers to the publishers and identify inefficiencies. A similar application of blockchain can also help customers verify whether marketing claims such as fair trade and 100% organic are accurate through recordkeeping of supply chain transactions.

Another area of implementation is for customer data management. Today, customer data is dispersed across multiple companies and brands. For example, one customer may participate in dozens of loyalty programs and share personal information to many parties. The fragmented nature makes it difficult for customers to aggregate points and make them large enough to be meaningful. Blockchain can potentially integrate multiple loyalty programs and at the same time reduce transactional friction in them.

Summary: It's Time for Human-Like Technologies to Take Off

The next tech has been in development for many decades but in a somewhat dormant state. In the next decade it will finally take off. Every foundation is in place with powerful computing, open-source software, high-speed Internet, cloud computing, ubiquitous mobile devices, and big data.

In its advanced state, the technology aims to emulate the highly contextual ways of human learning. Since birth, we have been trained to sense our surroundings and communicate with others. Life experience enriches our overall cognitive understanding of how the world works. It becomes a fundamental of machine learning, paving the way for AI. Computers are being trained the same way, with sensors and natural language processing. Big data provides the "life experience" enhancement. Machines try to emulate human imagination with AR and VR and replicate human social relationships with the IoT and blockchain.

The applications of the next tech for marketing are crucial. AI allows companies to perform real-time market research, which in turn empowers them to do quick personalization at scale. The contextual nature of the next tech enables an adaptive customer experience. Marketers can tailor content, offerings, and interactions to current customer emotions. And with distributed computing capabilities, the service delivery is in real-time at the point of demand.

REFLECTION QUESTIONS

- What next tech has your organization adopted today? What are some of the use cases in your organization?
- Have you thought about your organization's technology roadmap for the next five years? What are some of the opportunities and challenges?

CHAPTER 7

The New CX

Machines Are Cool, but Humans Are Warm

In 2015, the Henn-na Hotel in Japan opened what Guinness World Records officially recognized as the world's first robot-staffed hotel. Multilingual front-desk robots are equipped with facial recognition to help guests with check-in and checkout. A mechanical arm stores luggage at the reception. The robot concierge helps order taxis while the robot trolley brings baggage to rooms, and the housekeeping robot cleans the rooms. Most amenities are also high-tech. For instance, each room is equipped with a facial recognition door lock and in-room clothing steam closet.

Initially, the use of robots was a strategy of the hotelier to overcome the staff shortage in Japan. The expectation was that the minimum number of staff could run the hotel—keeping the labor cost down. But the robots created problems that frustrated guests, thus producing more work for the hotel staff to fix the issues. One example of a guest complaint was about an in-room tabletop robot that misunderstood snoring sounds for an inquiry and thus repeatedly woke up the sleeping guests. Consequently, the hotel cut back on automation and "fired" half of its robots.

This case highlights the limitation of full automation. Especially in the hospitality industry, which relies heavily on personal interactions, all-machine touchpoints may not be the best option after all. Not all tasks can be automated, as human connections are still indispensable. Robots are indeed cool, but people are proven to be warm. A combination of both will be the future of customer experience (CX).

The notion is supported by the fact that more and more customers are using a combination of online and offline channels. Research by McKinsey reveals that 44% of global customers adopted webrooming (search online and shop in-store) while 23% embraced showrooming (experience in-store and buy online). Other research by transcosmos in 10 major Asian cities discovered that most customers use both webrooming and showrooming for different product categories. This hybrid customer journey calls for an Omni approach to CX: high-tech yet high-touch.

Revisiting Customer Experience in the Digital World

CX is not a new idea. The concept of the Experience Economy was first postulated in 1998 by Pine and Gilmore, who argued that goods and services used to be the primary vehicle for innovation. But they have become so undifferentiated that premium pricing is no longer possible without a strategy upgrade.

A small distinction in product features may prevent customers from switching to a competitor, but it can hardly increase willingness-to-pay. Companies must move on to the next step in the progression of economic value: the experience. Using a theater as a metaphor, an experiential company engages with the customers memorably using goods as props and services as a stage.

The concept has gained more mainstream popularity with the rise of digitalization. First of all, Internet transparency has made it easy for customers to compare products and services, making commoditization happen faster. Thus, companies have to innovate in experiences beyond basic offerings. But most importantly, customers have been longing for genuine connection with brands, which paradoxically has become scarce in the connected era. As a result, companies today feel compelled to interact and engage with customers via the Internet and other digital technologies.

As products have become commoditized, businesses now turn their innovation focus to every touchpoint surrounding the products. The new ways to interact with a product are now more compelling than the product itself. The key to winning the competition no longer rests on the product but on how the customers evaluate, purchase, use, and recommend it. CX has essentially become a new effective way for companies to create and deliver more customer value.

In fact, CX is one of the primary drivers of business results. One-third of connected customers are willing to pay more for a great CX, according to a Salesforce survey. A PwC study also found that almost three out of four customers say that a great CX will make them stay loyal. And customers would pay a price premium of up to 16% for a better CX.

Keeping Track of Touchpoints: The 5*A*'s

Since the concept of CX is about augmenting the product innovation's narrow focus, it is vital to view it at a broader scope. CX is not only about the buying experience or customer service. In fact, CX starts long before customers buy the product and continues long after. It encompasses all the touchpoints customers might have with the product: brand communications, retail experience, salesforce interaction, product usage, customer service, and conversations with other customers. Companies must orchestrate all these touchpoints to deliver a seamless CX that is meaningful and memorable for the customers.

In Marketing 4.0, we introduced a framework to map these touchpoints and create a superior CX. The 5*A*'s customer path describes the journey customers take when they buy and consume products and services in the digital world (see Figure 7.1).

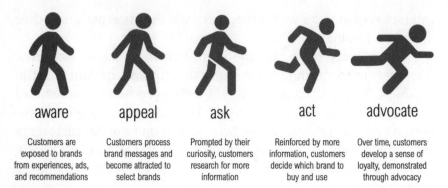

aware	appeal	ask	act	advocate
Customers are exposed to brands from experiences, ads, and recommendations	Customers process brand messages and become attracted to select brands	Prompted by their curiosity, customers research for more information	Reinforced by more information, customers decide which brand to buy and use	Over time, customers develop a sense of loyalty, demonstrated through advocacy

FIGURE 7.1   The 5*A*'s Customer Path

It is a flexible tool that applies to all industries. And when used to describe customer behavior, it draws a picture that is closer to the actual customer journey. Not only does it remain relevant today, but it also provides a strong foundation to see how to integrate humans and machines in the overall customer experience.

The 5*A*'s reflect that many seemingly personal customer purchase decisions are inherently social decisions. Customers experience difficulty in making their own decisions as the pace of life accelerates, content proliferates, and the attention span drops. So, they turn to their most trustworthy source of advice: friends and family. Customers now actively connect, ask questions about brands, and recommend them to others. As a result, the measure of customer loyalty also transforms from mere retention and repurchase to advocacy.

In the *aware* phase, customers are exposed to a long list of brands from experience, marketing communications, or advocacy of others. Aware of several brands, customers then process all the messages they are exposed to—creating short-term memory or amplifying long-term memory—and become attracted only to a shortlist of brands. This is the *appeal* phase. Prompted by their curiosity, customers usually follow up by actively researching the brands they are attracted to for more information from friends and family, from the media, or directly from the brands. This is the *ask* stage.

If convinced by further information in the *ask* stage, customers will decide to *act*. It is important to remember that the desired customer actions are not limited to purchase activities. After buying a brand, customers interact more deeply through consumption and usage as well as post-purchase services. Over time, customers may develop a sense of loyalty to the brand, which is reflected in retention, repurchase, and ultimately advocacy to others. This is the *advocate* stage.

The ultimate goal of every company is to drive customers from awareness to advocacy by providing excellent interactions throughout the journey. To accomplish this, companies must design each touchpoint carefully and determine when to use automation and when to use a personal human touch. Automation is usually useful when customers simply demand speed and efficiency, such as during reservation and payment. On the other hand, humans are still better at performing tasks requiring flexibility and contextual understanding, such as consultative and hospitality interactions.

Human and Machine in the New CX

The roles of humans and machines are equally crucial in a hybrid CX. Not only are they good at different things, but they also complement each other. The speed and efficiency of computers allow humans greater freedom to perform other activities that demand their imagination. Automation is a stepping-stone to take our creativity to the next level. In that sense, technology must be recognized as the enabler and accelerator of innovation. It serves the purpose for which technology was invented in the first place: as the liberator of human resources.

Before diving deeper into where machines and humans excel, we need to understand Moravec's paradox. Hans Moravec famously observed that it is relatively easy to make computers perform well on intelligence tests but almost impossible to give them the perception and mobility skills of a one-year-old child.

Reasoning, perceived to be a high-level capability in humans, can easily be taught to computers since it involves a lifetime of conscious learning. Because we know how it works, we can simply train machines with the same logic in a very straightforward process. Due to their higher computational power, they will learn it faster than we ever did and use it more reliably.

On the other hand, sensorimotor knowledge—our perception and response to surroundings—is harder to train into computers. It appears to be a low-level skill learned during early childhood when children effortlessly interact with people and the environment. It is about intuitively understanding other people's feelings and having empathy. Nobody knows how a child develops such capabilities as they mostly come from unconscious learning, built over millions of years of human evolution. Thus, it is difficult for us to teach what we do not understand.

AI scientists have been trying to reverse-engineer the unconscious learning by applying the conscious process. Computers analyze billions of faces and their unique characteristics to recognize each one and even predict the underlying emotion. The same goes for studying voices and languages. Results have been tremendous, but it takes decades to achieve them. In robotics, there has been limited success. Robots have managed to replicate our body movement as a response to external stimuli, but they have failed to reproduce the gracefulness.

Computers can easily surpass human capabilities that most people think are our greatest assets—logical thinking and reasoning. Conversely, what seems natural for humans to learn takes machines decades and enormous computer processing power to imitate. The skills that some people often take for granted—for instance, common sense and empathy—are the ones that differentiate us from computers. This is the paradox.

Variations in Handling Information

A key factor that defines the distinction between people and computers is the ability to handle information. There is an order in knowledge management known as the DIKW hierarchy: data, information, knowledge, and wisdom. Partly inspired by the play *The Rock* by T. S. Eliot, there have been numerous versions from different authors. We use a six-tier model by adding noise and insight into the DIKW framework (see Figure 7.2).

Data, information, and knowledge are the established domains of machines. Computers have become extremely good at processing disorganized data into meaningful information with speed and almost limitless capacity. The new resulting information is then added to a reservoir of related information and other known contexts to develop what is called knowledge. Computers organize and manage this wealth of knowledge in their storage and can retrieve it whenever needed. The quantitative nature and large volume of processing make machines ideal for this sort of work.

On the other hand, the three somewhat fuzzy and intuitive elements (noise, insight, and wisdom) are within the human realm. Noise is a distortion or deviation in data and can be a major distraction when grouping the data in structured clusters. An example of this is an outlier, which computers can quickly

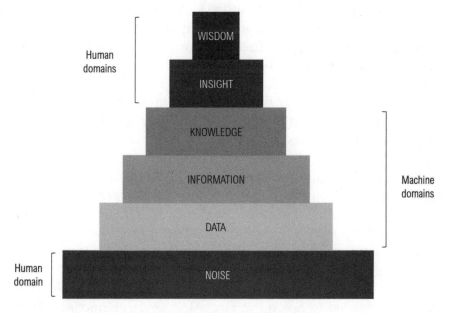

FIGURE 7.2   The Knowledge Management Hierarchy

identify as a significant deviation from other datasets. But an outlier can either be a valid variability or an error. And the only way to determine it is through a subjective judgment based on an understanding of the real world. This is where humans—businesspeople instead of data scientists—play a role in deciding whether to keep or filter out the outlier.

Human judgment in filtering the noises is vital. In some instances, insights can be found by discovering anomalies, in other words, the outlier data. Many market researchers or ethnographers frequently discover meaningful insights while watching unorthodox customer behaviors. They also often purposely observe extreme users at both ends of the normal distribution to find ideas out of the norms. Due to their rare occurrence, these unusual observations are usually deemed to have no statistical significance. The qualitative aspect of finding insights, beyond well-established knowledge, is best suited to humans' instinctive nature.

At the top of the hierarchy, there is wisdom, which is perhaps the most challenging virtue for machines to imitate from humans. It helps us make the right decisions with a mix of unbiased views, good judgment, and ethical considerations. No one knows exactly how we develop wisdom throughout our lives. But most people would agree that wisdom comes from a wealth of practical—not theoretical—experiences. In other words, humans learn from both the positive and negative implications of their past decisions, and over time their wisdom sharpens. Unlike in narrow machine learning, the process is very broad, covering all aspects of human lives.

In the area of market research, computers will help marketers to process information and create market simulation models. But at the end of the day, marketers need to use their wisdom to draw actionable insights and make the right call. Often, humans are required to override AI-recommended decisions.

A case in point is the airline incident involving David Dao, who was forcibly removed from a United flight in 2017. Four passengers had to leave to make room for airline personnel who urgently needed to board the aircraft. A revenue-maximization algorithm identified Dao as one of the passengers to get bumped due to his "least valuable" customer status—evaluated based on frequent flyer tier and fare class. A significant fact that the computer failed to recognize is that Dao is a doctor who needed to see his patient the following day. Carelessly following the computer bias without using empathy would often lead to the wrong decision. The rough handling of the situation also undermined the importance of human touch in CX.

Collaborative Human and Machine Thinking

Humans and machines can also collaborate in convergent and divergent thinking. Computers are known to have the ability of convergent thinking: identifying patterns and clusters in multiple unstructured datasets, which include not only text and numbers but also images and audiovisuals. In contrast, humans are good at divergent thinking: generating new ideas and exploring many potential solutions.

These complementary functions have enormous potential, for instance, in improving advertising effectiveness. Computers can run through millions of ads and discover correlations between basic creative dimensions (color scheme, copy, or layout) and the outcomes (awareness level, emotional appeal, or purchase conversion rates). It can be done either for pre-placement creative testing or historical ad performance audit. Chase, for example, uses AI from Persado for copywriting. In creative testing, the software managed to outperform human copywriters to get the highest click-through rates. The word choices were crafted from a massive database of words that have been rated for emotional appeal.

It should not be judged as a threat to brand managers and creative ad agencies. Thus far, no machines can replace humans in writing agency briefs or creating ad copy from scratch—that is, to craft brand positioning that resonates and then translate it into the right message. Computers are not ideal for designing a campaign that is authentic and novel, either. AI, however, can help optimize the ads by selecting better words, colors, and layout.

Human and Machine in Customer Interface

In the customer interface, humans and machines can go hand in hand, too. Typically, channel selection depends on customer tiering. Interactions with humans are generally reserved for hot prospects and most valuable customers due to the high cost-to-serve. Meanwhile, machines are employed to qualify leads as well as interact with low-cost-to-serve customers. The service segmentation allows businesses to control costs while at the same time managing risks.

Indeed, the use of AI for interactive purposes is risky. Microsoft's now-defunct chatbot Tay illustrates this. Learning and responding from abusive tweets from provocative users, Tay began posting equally offensive messages via Twitter. The bot was retired after only 16 hours since launch. Google experienced a similar problem when its image recognition algorithm labeled a user's black friends as gorillas. The company fixed the algorithm by eliminating the word *gorillas* from its labels altogether. The insensitivity of AI is one of the biggest threats to manage.

Computers are a good fit only for predictable inquiries and programmable tasks. Solutions such as self-service kiosks and chatbots handle only basic transactions and queries. People are more flexible across a broader range of topics, and therefore better suited to perform in a consultative role. Their superior contextual understanding allows humans to adapt to unpredictable circumstances and unusual customer scenarios, beyond standard procedures.

Software company HubSpot, for instance, uses a chatbot to capture and nurture leads in its top and middle sales funnel. But the company assigns a sales force to do consultative selling for qualified leads and a high-touch team for onboarding. For post-sales, the company returns to the chatbot to answer simple queries.

Above all, humans are warm and friendly. For any tasks that require empathy, human-to-human connection offers the best solutions. Even some companies that have already installed high-tech customer management solutions still rely on people's social skills for service deliveries. Take Marriott with M Live, its social listening center. When social listening identifies a missed opportunity in one of Marriott's properties—for example, a couple on honeymoon—the command center notifies the respective hotel so that they can surprise the guests.

Understanding what automation and a human touch can deliver is the first important step to designing an excellent Omni CX (see Figure 7.3). And it is often not about selecting one or the other. Businesses need to drop the "machines replacing humans" mindset or risk missing an opportunity to optimize

MACHINE   HUMAN

Efficient at processing **data**,   Capable of screening out **noise**,
extracting **information**, and   drawing out **insight**, and
managing **knowledge**   developing **wisdom**

Adept at **convergent, structured**   Skilled in **divergent thinking** and
thinking and discovering **patterns** finding **out-of-the-box** solutions

Excellent at using **logical** thinking   Great at using **empathy** to create
that follows specific **algorithms**   a **connection** that **resonates**

Reliable for **repetitive** and   Flexible for tasks that demand
programmable tasks at speed   **contextual understanding** and
and scale   **commonsense reasoning**

FIGURE 7.3 Combining the Strengths of Machines and Humans

their operations. In truth, humans and computers should coexist and build on each other's strengths in most touchpoints. Thus, the next step involves reimagining and redesigning the customer path to harness the full power of the collaboration (see Chapter 11).

Leveraging the Next Tech for the New CX: A Checklist

To ensure a smooth collaboration, the next-generation marketers must have a working knowledge of technologies, especially those that enhance marketing activities. A group of technologies that marketers often use is called marketing technology (martech). There are seven most common use cases of martech across the customer path.

Advertising

Advertising is an approach to communicate brand messages to intended mass audiences through various paid media. In a world where attention is scarce, advertising can be seen as intrusive. Relevance is critical. Thus, the most common use case of technology in advertising is for audience targeting. Companies can optimize effectiveness by finding the right segment, which will eventually improve the ad's perceived relevance.

Technology also helps marketers to create accurate portrayals of audience segments or personas, which lead to better ad creation. As one size often does not fit all in advertising, AI is capable of quickly producing multiple ad creatives with different combinations of copies and visuals. Also known as dynamic creative, it is essential for personalization purposes.

The personalization is not limited merely to the ad messages but also applies to the media placement. Contextual advertising allows ads to appear at the right moment in the right medium automatically. For example, a car ad may appear on the screen of a user who is researching the next car to buy on a review site. As the ad messages are aligned with their current areas of interest, the ads typically have a better response rate (see Chapter 10).

Finally, another important use of technology in advertising is for programmatic media buying. A programmatic platform enables advertisers to automate the buying and management of paid media space. Since it is a consolidated purchase with automated bidding, programmatic advertising has proven useful to optimize media spend.

Content Marketing

Content marketing has been a buzzword in recent years, and it is being touted as a subtle alternative to advertising in the digital economy. Content is considered less intrusive than ads. It uses a mix of entertainment, education, and inspiration to attract attention without the hard sell. A fundamental principle in content marketing is to clearly define the audience group so that marketers can design content that is interesting, relevant, and useful. Thus, audience targeting is even more vital in content marketing.

Analytics is useful to track and analyze the audience's needs and interests. It allows content marketers to generate and curate articles, videos, infographics, and other content that the audience is most likely to consume. AI also enables this laborious process to be automated.

With predictive analytics, content marketers can even envision every single customer journey on their website. So instead of showing static content based on a predetermined flow, marketers can offer dynamic content. In other words, every website visitor will see different content depending on their past behaviors and preferences. It allows content marketers to walk customers through their path to purchase. That way, the conversion rate from visitors to leads to buyers can be significantly boosted, leading to optimized performance. Amazon and Netflix provide personalized pages to drive users closer to desired actions.

Direct Marketing

Direct marketing is a more targeted tactic for selling products and services. In contrast to mass media advertising, direct marketing is about the individualized distribution of sales offerings with intermediaries, typically using media such as mail and email. In most cases, potential customers subscribe to a direct marketing channel in the hope of getting promotional offers and the latest updates—known as permission marketing.

A direct marketing message should feel personal for it not to be perceived as spam. Thus, the message copy should be tailored to a specific person with the help of AI. But perhaps the most important use case for direct marketing is the product recommendation system, which is an everyday staple in e-commerce. With the engine, marketers can predict which products customers would most likely buy based on past histories and generate the offers accordingly. Since personalization of offers is vital, and the volume can be massive, the use of automated workflow in direct marketing is a must.

And as the offers always have a specific call to action, campaign success can be both predicted and measured by analyzing the conversion rates. Hence, the use of technology can also be beneficial for forecasting and campaign analytics. The constant tracking of responses will enable the algorithms to improve over time.

Sales Customer Relationship Management (Sales CRM)

In the sales department, automation technology can bring significant cost savings as well as facilitate scalability. Some parts of the lead management process, especially at the top of the funnel, can be delegated to chatbots. With chatbots, lead capture can be conversational and use less formal forms. The programmable nature of the lead qualification also makes it ideal for chatbots to take over this process. Some advanced bots can also automate the lead-nurturing process—or the middle sales funnel—by responding to prospect inquiries and providing contextually relevant information smartly.

Marketing technology has also grown in the area of account management. Across industry verticals, salespeople spend a significant amount of time on non-selling activities and administrative tasks. With sales CRM, account information including contact histories and sales opportunities is organized automatically, allowing the salesforce to focus on the actual selling activities. The massive data collected throughout the lead management process will equip the human salesforce with the right information to take deals forward.

Forecasting is also problematic for many businesses, as most salespeople rely on intuition to evaluate every sales lead. The issue is that every salesperson has a different quality of intuition, making the overall forecast flawed. Predictive analytics enables the sales team to make more accurate forecasts and allow them to prioritize sales opportunities better.

Distribution Channel

The next tech also has various use cases for improving the distribution channel. The most popular, especially after the COVID-19 pandemic, is for contactless frontline interactions at retailers. Aside from reducing costs, self-service interfaces and frontline robots are more favorable for simple interactions such as banking transactions, food order taking, and airport check-in. The pandemic outbreak could also finally push drone delivery to take off. In China, JD.com became the first to deliver goods by drone to remote areas during the lockdown.

Advanced technology can also ensure a frictionless customer experience. Retailers are also among the first to experiment with sensors. Amazon, which continues to expand its brick-and-mortar presence, tried out biometrics payment systems in several Whole Foods locations. In China, customers can check out at retailers by posing in front of cashiers equipped with a facial recognition device that is linked to Alipay or WeChat Pay.

The use of IoT is also becoming more popular. In smart stores outfitted with sensors, visitor movement can be analyzed, and therefore the actual customer journey can be easily mapped. Thus, retailers can make adjustments to store layouts for improved experience. With IoT, retailers can also pinpoint exactly where each customer is at any given time, allowing for precise location-based marketing in every aisle and shelf.

With a mix of the next tech, channel players can empower customers for a pre-purchase virtual experience. Augmented reality (AR) and voice search, for example, have been used for product feature highlight and in-store navigation in Sam's Club. Virtual reality (VR) makes it possible for customers to browse retail stores without having to go there. Prada, for instance, was the first luxury brand to use VR to replace retail experience during the pandemic.

Product and Service

Marketing technology is not only valuable for improving customer interactions but also for enhancing the core products and services. Trends toward online shopping and personalization give rise to the concept of mass customization and co-creation. Everyone wants products custom-made for them with their initials, color choices, and sizes that fit their body measurements. From Gillette to Levi's to Mercedes-Benz, companies are extending their product lineup by offering customization options.

Dynamic pricing should also be in place to match the vast customization possibilities. In the services business, the role of custom pricing is even more apparent. Insurance companies provide the option to select the coverage that suits individual customer needs, which will be reflected in the pricing. Airlines may determine the pricing based on multiple variables, not only general information, such as current demand level and route competition, but also individual travelers' customer lifetime value. Technology also enables the "everything-as-a-service" business model for previously big-ticket purchases such as enterprise software or a car.

Predictive analytics can also be useful for product development. Companies can assess the risk of current plans and estimate market acceptance. For instance, PepsiCo used analytics provided by Black Swan to analyze beverage conversations trends and predict what products in the pipeline have the highest likelihood of success (see Chapter 9).

Service Customer Relationship Management (Service CRM)

The use of chatbots is popular not only for managing the sales funnel but also for responding to service inquiries. With a chatbot, a company can provide 24/7 customer service access and offer common resolutions instantly, which are crucial in the digital world. And the company can ensure better consistency and integration across multiple channels such as websites, social media, and mobile applications. But most importantly, chatbot reduces the workload of customer service reps for handling simple tasks.

For more complex inquiries, the chatbot can seamlessly transfer the ticket to customer service agents. The integration with the CRM database can significantly enhance the performance of the agents by equipping them with a list of past interactions and other relevant information. The agents can then determine the best resolutions for customer problems.

Another important use case is related to churn detection. Businesses have been using social listening to track and measure customer sentiments online. But with a predictive analytics engine embedded in the social listening platform, companies can also predict the likelihood of customer churn and prevent it.

There is no doubt that businesses must make the most of marketing technology. The major question for business leaders, however, is how to determine which technologies to implement as not all will fit the overall corporate strategies. The next challenge is to integrate various use cases into a seamless and frictionless CX (see Figure 7.4). One thing for sure is that with

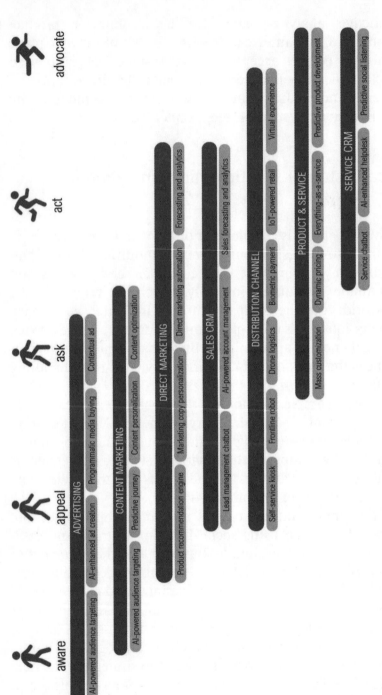

FIGURE 7.4   Marketing Technology Use Cases in the New CX

technology, marketers will leave the science part of marketing to machines and focus on the art.

Summary: Machines Are Cool, But Humans Are Warm

Customer experience is the new way to win the highly contested markets. Interactive and immersive experiences that used to be on the periphery are now more important than the core products and services. To create a compelling and superior CX across touchpoints from awareness to advocacy, leveraging advanced technologies is a must.

In marketing, the use cases of the next tech spread across seven different touchpoints: advertising, content marketing, direct marketing, sales, channel, offering, and service. Technology is primarily useful to analyze data and uncover insights about specific target markets. Finding the optimal configuration, for example, in media buying and pricing, is another area where marketing technology has proven effective. The predictive power of AI is valuable for sales forecasting, product recommendation, and potential churn detection. AI also allows marketers to personalize products and services at scale and speed.

But the role of human touch must never be overlooked, as it will counterbalance the speed and efficiency that technology provides with wisdom, flexibility, and empathy. The unprecedented access to insights and time savings from automation will enable marketers to step up their creativity. While machines are more reliable for programmable workflow, people with their intuition and common sense are far more flexible. But, most importantly, humans are truly irreplaceable when it comes to building heartfelt connections.

REFLECTION QUESTIONS

- Map the customer journey in your organization. What are the most critical touchpoints based on your experience?
- What improvements can marketing technology bring to the most critical touchpoints? How do you plan to implement them?

PART IV

New Tactics Leveraging Marketing Tech

CHAPTER 8

Data-Driven Marketing

Building a Data Ecosystem for Better Targeting

In 2012, an article by Charles Duhigg in *The New York Times Magazine* about Target predicting the pregnancy of a teenager made a headline. The father of the teen was angry to learn that his daughter had been receiving promotional coupons for baby items from the retailer. He thought that the mail was misdirected, and Target was encouraging her to get pregnant. After a conversation with her, he learned that she was indeed expecting.

A year before the event, Target had built an algorithm to predict the likelihood that a woman shopper was pregnant according to the items she bought. The retailer had assigned a unique ID to every shopper and connected it to all demographic information and the shopping history. Big data analytics had revealed a specific consumption pattern for actual pregnant women, which could be used to predict future purchases of shoppers that matched the pattern. The company had even attempted to predict the due date based on the timing of the shopping. All these efforts would be useful to determine who would get which mailed coupons and when.

The story is an excellent example of companies leveraging data ecosystems to make more informed decisions. Data-driven marketing is the first step in implementing Marketing 5.0.

By having an analytics engine, brands can predict what their potential customers are more likely to buy next based on past purchases. That way, brands can send personalized offers and run custom campaigns. Today's digital infrastructure makes it possible to do those things not only to a handful of market segments but also to individual customers one by one.

For more than 20 years, marketers have been dreaming of having this capability to create truly personalized marketing. Don Peppers and Martha Rogers are the early proponents of one-to-one marketing, which is a highly coveted practice. The "segments of one" is considered the ultimate segmentation method, and the digital technologies implementation in marketing all boils down to enabling it.

The Segments of One

The market is heterogeneous, and every customer is unique. That is why marketing always starts with segmentation and targeting. Based on market understanding, companies can design strategies and tactics to take on the market. The more micro the segmentation, the more the marketing approach will resonate, but the harder the execution will be.

The segmentation approach itself has evolved since it was conceptualized in the 1950s. There are four methods to conduct a market segmentation: geographic, demographic, psychographic, and behavioral.

Four Methods of Segmentation

Marketers always start with geographic segmentation, which is to divide the market by countries, regions, cities, and locations. Once they realize that geographic segments are too broad, they add demographic variables: age, gender, occupation, and socio-economic class. "Young, middle-class women living in Illinois" or "affluent New York Baby Boomers" are examples of segment names with geographic-demographic variables.

On the one hand, geographic and demographic segmentation methods are top-down and thus very easy to understand. More importantly, they are actionable. Companies know exactly where to find and how to identify the segments. On the other hand, the segments are less meaningful as people with the same demographic profile and who live in the same locations might have different purchase preferences and behavior. Moreover, they are relatively static, which means that one customer can only be classified in one segment across all products. In reality, the customer decision journey differs by category and lifecycle.

As market research becomes common, marketers use a more bottom-up approach. Instead of breaking down the market, they cluster customers with similar preferences and behavior into groups according to their responses to survey questions. Despite bottom-up, the grouping is exhaustive, which means every single customer in the population gets into a segment. Well-known methods include psychographic and behavioral segmentation.

In psychographic segmentation, customers are clustered based on their personal beliefs and values as well as interests and motivation. Resulting segment names are usually self-explanatory, such as "social climber" or "experiencer." A psychographic segment also demonstrates an attitude toward a specific product or service feature, for example, "quality-oriented" or "cost-conscious." The psychographic segmentation provides a good proxy for purchase behavior. One's values and attitudes are the drivers of their decision making.

An even more accurate method is behavioral segmentation, as it retrospectively groups customers based on actual past behavior. The behavioral segments may include names that reflect purchase frequency and amount, such as "frequent flyer" and "top spender." It can also show customer loyalty and depth of interaction with names such as "loyal fan" or "brand switcher" or "first-time buyer."

The techniques are highly meaningful as the segments precisely reflect clusters of customers with different needs. That way, marketers can tailor their strategies to each group. Psychographic and behavioral segmentation, however, is less actionable.

Segments with names such as "adventure addict" or "bargain hunter" are only useful to design advertising creative or *pull* marketing. In *push* marketing, however, it is harder for sales-people and other frontline staff to identify these segments when they meet the customers.

Segmentation should be top-down and bottom-up. In other words, it should be both meaningful and actionable. Thus, it should combine all four variables: geographic, demographic, psychographic, and behavioral. With psychographic and behavioral segmentation, marketers can cluster customers into meaningful groups and then add the geographic and demographic profile to each segment to make it actionable.

Developing a Persona

The resulting brief fictional depiction of a customer segment with all four variables is called a *persona*. Here is an example of a persona:

> *John is a 40-year-old digital marketing manager who has 15 years of experience and currently works for a major consumer-packaged-goods company. He is responsible for designing, developing, and implementing marketing campaigns across digital media and reports to the marketing director.*
>
> *The director measures John's performance by the overall brand awareness and online conversation rates in e-commerce channels. Aside from striving to improve performance based on the metrics, John is also highly cost-conscious and believes that digital marketing spending should be as efficient as possible.*
>
> *To manage everything, John works with his staff and also digital marketing agencies. He has a team of five people reporting to him, each handling different media channels. He has contracts with an SEO agency that helps manage the website as well as a social media agency that helps with content marketing.*

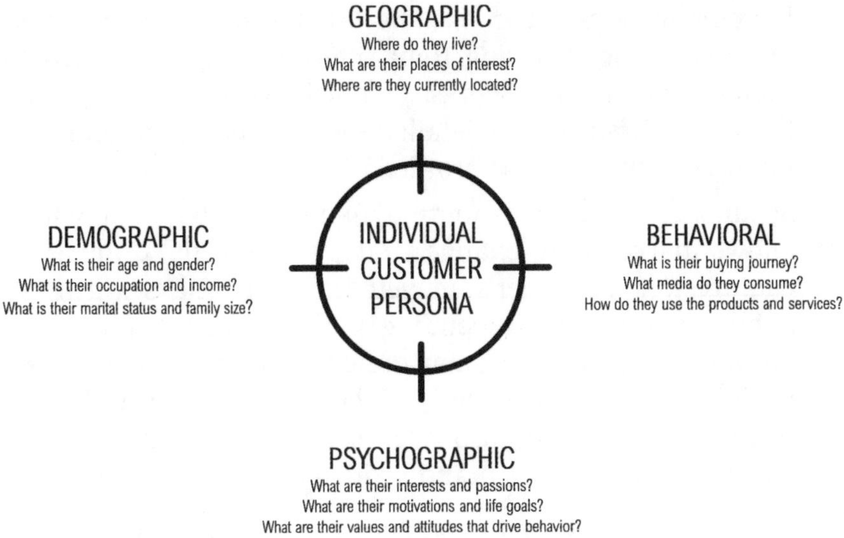

GEOGRAPHIC
Where do they live?
What are their places of interest?
Where are they currently located?

DEMOGRAPHIC
What is their age and gender?
What is their occupation and income?
What is their marital status and family size?

INDIVIDUAL
CUSTOMER
PERSONA

BEHAVIORAL
What is their buying journey?
What media do they consume?
How do they use the products and services?

PSYCHOGRAPHIC
What are their interests and passions?
What are their motivations and life goals?
What are their values and attitudes that drive behavior?

FIGURE 8.1 Segments-of-One Customer Profiling

The example is a persona that can be useful for a digital marketing agency or a digital marketing automation software company looking to acquire new clients. It lays out the profile of the fictionalized prospect and, most importantly, what matters to him. Thus, the persona can be useful in designing the right marketing strategy.

Segmenting and profiling customers has been a staple for marketers. But the rise of big data opens up new possibilities for marketers to collect new types of market data and perform micro-segmentation (see Figure 8.1). Customer database and market surveys are no longer the only sources of customer information. Media data, social data, web data, point-of-sale (POS) data, Internet of Things (IoT) data, and engagement data can all enrich the profiles of the customers. The challenge for companies is to create a data ecosystem that integrates all these data.

Once the data ecosystem is set up, marketers can enhance their existing marketing segmentation practice in two ways:

1. Big data empowers marketers to segment the market into the most granular unit: an individual customer. Marketers can essentially create a real persona for each customer. Based on

it, companies can then execute one-to-one or segments-of-one marketing, tailoring their offerings and campaigns to each customer. And thanks to enormous computing power, there is no limit to how detailed the persona can be and how many customers can be profiled.

2. Segmentation becomes more dynamic with big data, which allows marketers to change strategy on the fly. Companies can track a customer's movement from one segment to another in real-time, depending on the different contexts. An air traveler, for instance, may prefer business-class seats for a business trip while choosing an economy class for his leisure travel. Marketers can also track if a marketing intervention has managed to shift a brand-switcher into a loyal customer.

It is important to note that despite the enhancement, traditional segmentation is still beneficial. It facilitates simple market understanding. Putting a descriptive label on a customer group helps marketers wrap their heads around the market. It cannot be achieved with too many segments-of-one since human computational power is not as strong as a computer's. The easy-to-understand labeling is also helpful to mobilize people within the organization toward the overall brand vision.

Setting Up Data-Driven Marketing

Great marketing usually comes from great market insights. Over the past few decades, marketers have perfected the way they conduct market research to uncover information that their competitors do not have. A combination of qualitative research and quantitative survey becomes the norm for every marketer before beginning any marketing planning cycle.

In the last decade, marketers have also become obsessed with collecting a robust customer database to facilitate better customer relationship management (CRM). The availability of big data has led to the rise of data-driven marketing. Marketers believe that hidden beneath the massive volume of data are real-time insights that can empower them to boost marketing like never before. And they began to wonder how to merge two siloed sets of information from market research and analytics into a unified data management platform.

Despite the promise, not many companies have figured out the best way to do data-driven marketing. Most of them end up with a huge technology investment but have yet to realize the full benefits of the data ecosystem. The failures of data-driven marketing practice are down to three primary reasons:

1. Companies often treat data-driven marketing as an IT project. When embarking on the journey, they focus too much on selecting the software tools, making an infrastructure investment, and hiring data scientists. Data-driven marketing should be a marketing project. The IT infrastructure follows the marketing strategy, not the other way around. It does not merely mean making the marketing people sponsors of the project. Marketers should be the ones defining and designing the entire data-driven marketing process. As many market researchers believe, a larger volume of data does not always mean better insights. The key is to understand what to look for in the oceans of information by having clear marketing objectives.

2. Big data analytics is often considered the silver bullet that unravels every customer insight and solves every marketing problem. Big data is not a substitute for traditional market research methods, especially the high-touch ones, such as ethnography, usability testing, or taste testing. In fact, big data and market research should complement and augment each other because data-driven marketing needs both. Market research is carried out on a regular cycle for specific and narrow objectives. On the other hand, big data is collected and analyzed in real time to improve marketing on-the-go.

3. Big data analytics brings so much promise of automation that companies think that once set up, it can be on autopilot. The expectation is that marketers can pour large datasets into the black box called algorithm and get instant answers

to their questions. In reality, marketers still need to be very hands-on in data-driven marketing. And although a machine can spot data patterns that no human can, it always takes a marketer with experience and contextual knowledge to filter and interpret the patterns. More importantly, actionable insights require marketers who will design new offers or campaigns, albeit with the help of computers.

Step 1: Define the Data-Driven Marketing Objectives

It seems like a no-brainer to start any project with clear goals. But too often, a data-driven marketing project is launched with the objectives as an afterthought. Moreover, most data projects become too ambitious because marketers want to accomplish everything at once. As a result, the projects become too complicated, proven results become challenging to achieve, and companies eventually give up.

The use cases of data-driven marketing are indeed aplenty and broad in scope. With big data, marketers can discover new product and service ideas and estimate market demand. Companies can also create customized products and services and personalize the customer experience. Calculating the right pricing and setting up a dynamic pricing model also requires a data-driven approach.

Aside from assisting marketers in defining what to offer, big data is also useful to determine how to deliver. In marketing communications, marketers use big data for audience targeting, content creation, and media selection. It is valuable for push marketing, such as channel selection and lead generation. It is also common to use data for after-sales service and customer retention. Big data is often used to predict churn and determine service recovery measures.

Despite abundant use cases, it is crucial to narrow the focus to one or two objectives when embarking on a data-driven marketing endeavor. By nature, people are wary of things they do not understand, and the technicalities of data-driven marketing

'What to offer'

• Discover new product and service ideas
• Estimate market demand for products and services
• Recommend the next purchase
• Create custom products and services
• Personalize the customer experience
• Determine the right pricing for new products
• Enable dynamic pricing policy

'How to offer'

• Target and locate the right audience
• Determine the right marketing message and content
• Select the right media mix for communications
• Select the channel mix to go to market
• Profile customer for lead generation and nurturing
• Design customer service tiers
• Identify potential complaint and customer churn

FIGURE 8.2   Examples of Data-Driven Marketing Objectives

can be the intimidating unknown for everyone in the organization from top to bottom.

Narrow goals are easier to communicate and therefore help mobilize people in the organization, especially those who are skeptical. It helps align various units, draw their commitment, and ensure accountability. Focused goals also force marketers to think about the most effective performance leverage and prioritize their effort on it. When marketers choose the objective with the biggest impact, companies can get meaningful quick wins and hence early buy-in from everyone.

By setting clear goals, the data-driven marketing initiative becomes a measurable and accountable initiative (see Figure 8.2). The insights generated from data analysis will also be more actionable and lead to specific marketing improvement efforts.

Step 2: Identify Data Requirements and Availability

In the digital era, the volume of data is growing exponentially. Not only is the level of detail deepening, but the variety is also widening. However, not all of the data are valuable and relevant. After companies zoom in on the objectives, they must start identifying the right data to collect and analyze.

There is no one right way to classify big data. But one of the practical ways is to categorize based on the source:

1. Social data, which includes all the information that social media users share, such as location, demographic profile, and interests

2. Media data, which includes audience measurement for traditional media, such as television, radio, print, and cinema

3. Web traffic data, which includes all logs generated by users navigating the web, such as page views, searches, and purchases

4. POS and transaction data, which include all records of transactions made by customers, such as location, amount, credit card information, purchases, timing, and sometimes customer ID

5. IoT data, which includes all information collected by connected devices and sensors, such as location, temperature, humidity, the proximity of other devices, and vital signs

6. Engagement data, which includes all the direct touchpoints that companies make with customers, such as call center data, email exchange, and chat data

Marketers need to develop a data collection plan that lays out every piece of data that must be acquired to achieve the predetermined objective. A data matrix is a useful tool that maps the required data against the goal. Looking at the data matrix horizontally, marketers can determine if they have enough data to accomplish the objective. To have valid insights, they need data triangulation: having multiple data sources that contribute to a convergent understanding. Looking at the data matrix vertically also helps marketers understand what information they need to extract from each data source (see Figure 8.3).

Some of the data types mentioned in the numbered list previously, such as transaction and engagement data, are internal and accessible for marketers. However, not all internal data is ready for use. Depending on how well organized and maintained the records, data cleansing may be required. It includes fixing

OBJECTIVES	REQUIRED ANALYSIS	DATA SOURCES					
		Social data	Media data	Web data	POS data	IoT data	Engagement data
Select the right media mix for marketing communications	Audience profiling and targeting	X	X	X	X	X	X
	Customer journey mapping	X	X	X	X	X	X
	Content analysis	X		X			
	Media habit	X	X	X			
	Inbound marketing effectiveness	X		X	X		X

 Data triangulation

Focus of analysis

FIGURE 8.3 Data Matrix Framework

inaccurate datasets, consolidating duplicates, and dealing with incomplete records.

Other datasets, such as social and media data, are external data and must be acquired via third-party providers. Some data can also come from value chain partners, such as suppliers, logistics companies, retailers, and outsourcing companies.

Step 3: Build an Integrated Data Ecosystem

Most data-driven marketing initiatives begin as ad-hoc, agile projects. In the long run, however, data-driven marketing must be a routine operation. To make sure the data collection effort gets maintained and continuously updated, companies must build a data ecosystem that integrates all the external and internal data.

The biggest challenge for data integration is to find a common denominator across all data sources. The most ideal is to integrate the data at the individual customer level, allowing for the segments-of-one marketing. Good recordkeeping practices ensure that every captured dataset about the customer is always tied to unique customer IDs.

While it is straightforward for internal data sources, using customer IDs for external data is a challenging, albeit doable, exercise. For instance, social data can be integrated with the customer ID and purchase data if the customer logs into e-commerce websites using their social media accounts, such as Google or Facebook. Another example of data integration is using a customer loyalty app to connect to smart beacon sensors. Whenever a customer carrying his mobile phone is near a sensor, for instance, in a retail aisle, the sensor records the movement. It is useful to track the customer journey in physical locations.

However, sometimes it is not possible to tie everything to an individual customer ID, primarily due to privacy concerns. A compromise solution is to use a specific demographic segmentation variable as the common denominator. For example, the "18-to-34-year-old male customer" segment name can be the unique ID to consolidate every information item from every data source about the particular demographic.

Every dynamic dataset should be stored in a single data management platform, which enables marketers to capture, store, manage, and analyze the data comprehensively. Any new data-driven marketing projects with new objectives should continue to use the same platform, enabling a richer data ecosystem, which is beneficial if the company decides to use machine learning to automate analysis.

Summary: Building Data Ecosystem for Better Targeting

The rise of big data has changed the face of market segmentation and targeting. The breadth and depth of customer data are increasing exponentially. Media data, social data, web data, POS data, IoT data, and engagement data can all make up a rich profile of individual customers, allowing marketers to perform segments-of-one marketing.

In the digital era, the problem is no longer the lack of data but rather identifying the ones that matter. That is why data-driven marketing must always start by defining specific, narrow objectives. Based on the goals, marketers acquire relevant datasets and integrate them into a data management platform that is connected to an analytics or machine learning engine. The resulting insights can lead to sharper marketing offers and campaigns.

Data-driven marketing, however, should never be embarked on as an IT initiative. A strong marketing leadership team should spearhead the project and align the company's resources, including IT support. The involvement of every marketer in the organization is imperative, as data-driven marketing is not a silver bullet and will never be run on autopilot.

REFLECTION QUESTIONS

- Think about how better data management can improve marketing practices in your organization. What is the low-hanging fruit?
- How do you segment the market for your products and services? Create a roadmap to implement segments-of-one marketing in your organization data.

CHAPTER 9

Predictive Marketing

Anticipating Market Demand
with Proactive Action

Following the 2001 Major League Baseball season, the Oakland Athletics lost three key players due to free agency. Under pressure to replace the free agents with limited budgets, the then–general manager Billy Beane turned to analytics to assemble a strong team for the following season. Instead of using traditional scouts and insider information, the A's used sabermetrics—analysis of in-game statistics.

With analytics, the A's discovered that underrated metrics such as on-base percentage and slugging percentage could be better predictors of performance compared to more conventional offensive stats. Since no other teams are recruiting players with these qualities, the insights allowed the A's to recruit undervalued players and maintain relatively modest payroll. The remarkable story was documented in Michael Lewis's book and Bennett Miller's movie, *Moneyball*.

It attracted the attention of other sports clubs and sports investors around the world. John Henry, the owner of the Boston Red Sox and Liverpool Football Club, was one of them. Mathematical models were used for the rebuilding of Liverpool. The soccer club, despite its fantastic history, was struggling to compete in the English Premier League. Based on analytics, the club appointed manager Jürgen Klopp and recruited some players onto the team that would go on to win the 2018–2019 UEFA Champions League and the 2019–2020 English Premier League.

These stories epitomize the essence of predictive analytics. It allows companies to anticipate market movement before it occurs. Traditionally, marketers rely on descriptive statistics that explain past behavior and use their intuition to make smart guesses on what will happen next. In predictive analytics, most of the analysis is carried out by artificial intelligence (AI). Past data are loaded into a machine learning engine to reveal specific patterns, which is called a predictive model. By entering new data into the model, marketers can predict future outcomes, such as who is likely to buy, which product will sell, or what campaign will work. Since predictive marketing relies heavily on data, companies usually build the capability upon the data ecosystem they have previously established (see Chapter 8).

With foresight, companies can be more proactive with forward-looking investments. For instance, companies can predict whether new clients with currently small transaction amounts will turn out to be major accounts. That way, the decision to invest resources to grow the specific clients can be optimal. Before allocating too many resources into new product development, companies can also use predictive analytics to help with the filtering of ideas. All in all, predictive analytics leads to a better return on marketing investment.

Predictive modeling is not a new subject. For many years, data-driven marketers build regression models to find causality between actions and results. But with machine learning, computers do not need a predetermined algorithm from data scientists to start uncovering patterns and models on their own. The resulting predictive models coming out of a machine learning "black box" are often beyond human comprehension and reasoning. And this is a good thing. Marketers are now no longer restricted to past biases, assumptions, and limited views of the world when predicting the future.

Predictive Marketing Applications

Predictive analytics uses and analyzes past historical data. But it is beyond descriptive statistics, which is useful for retrospectively reporting past company results and explaining the reasons behind them. Companies with a vision of the future want to know more than just what happened in the past. It is also beyond real-time analytics that is used for providing a quick response in contextual marketing (Chapter 10) or testing marketing activities in agile marketing (Chapter 12).

Predictive analytics examines past behaviors of customers to assess the likelihood that they will exhibit similar or related actions in the future. It discovers subtle patterns in the big data and recommends the best course of action. Very future-oriented, it helps marketers to stay ahead of the curve, prepare marketing responses ahead of time, and influence the outcome.

Predictive analytics is critical for proactive and preventive measures, which is perfect for marketing planning purposes. With predictive analytics, marketers have a powerful tool at their disposal to enhance decision making (see Figure 9.1). Marketers can now determine which market scenario is likely to happen and which customers are worthwhile to pursue. They can also assess which marketing actions and strategies have the highest likelihood of success before launching them—significantly reducing the risks of failure.

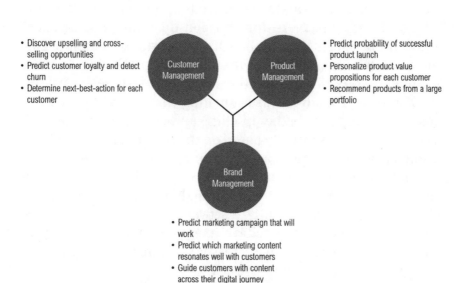

FIGURE 9.1   Predictive Marketing Applications

Predictive Customer Management

Targeting and serving a customer without knowing the future income the customer will bring is a marketing investment nightmare. Marketers need to decide whether to spend customer acquisition and service costs—for advertising, direct marketing, customer support, and account management—to get and nurture the customer. Predictive analytics can help marketers make this decision better by estimating the value of a customer.

The predictive model used for customer management purposes is called the customer equity model. It measures customer lifetime value (CLV), which is the present value of projected net income generated from a customer during the entire relationship with the company. It provides a long-term, forward-looking view on the return of investment, which is critical because most customers might not be profitable in the first or second year due to the high customer acquisition costs.

The concept is most relevant for business-to-business (B2B) companies and services companies with long-term customer relationships, such as banks and telcos. Companies serving corporate clients have massive customer acquisition spending, especially for trade shows and salesforce costs. Similarly, banks spend a lot of money on advertising and sign-up bonuses while telcos are well-known for their mobile device subsidies to acquire customers. For companies in these sectors, the marketing costs are too high for one-time transactions and short-term relationships.

The role of analytics in estimating the CLV is to predict a customer's response to the upselling and cross-selling offerings. The algorithms are usually based on the historical data of which products were purchased as a bundle by customers with similar profiles. Moreover, marketers can predict the length of relationship with each customer. Predictive analytics can detect customer churn and, more importantly, discover reasons for churn. Thus, companies can develop effective retention strategies to prevent customer attrition. For those reasons, predictive analytics not only forecasts but also improves CLV.

Once the customers are profiled and their CLVs are calculated, marketers can implement next-best-action (NBA) marketing. It is a customer-centric approach in which marketers have orchestrated a clear, step-by-step action plan for each customer. In other words, it is a marketing plan for the "segments of one." With multichannel interactions from digital marketing to the salesforce, marketers guide each customer from pre-sales to sales to post-sales service. In each step, predictive analytics can help marketers determine which move they should make next: send more marketing collateral, do a product demo, or send a team to make a sales call.

In a simpler form, businesses can also perform CLV-based customer tiering, which is essentially a resource allocation tool. The leveling dictates how much money companies should allocate to acquiring and retaining a customer in a particular tier. Marketers can prioritize which customers to build a relationship with and drive them to higher levels over time.

It also becomes the basis for the different customer interfaces that companies provide to different customers. That is, customers with higher profit contribution will get access to a dedicated customer support team while others will get access to an automated digital interface (see Chapter 11).

Predictive Product Management

Marketers can utilize predictive analytics across the product lifecycle. The predictions can start early in the product development ideation. Based on an analysis of what attributes work in already-marketed products, businesses can develop new products with a combination of all the right features.

This predictive marketing practice allows the product development team to avoid repeatedly going back to the drawing board. Having a product design and prototype that have a higher chance of success in market tests and actual launch will save marketers a significant part of the development costs. Moreover, external information on what is trending and what will resonate with potential buyers also feeds into the algorithms. It allows marketers to be proactive and leverage trends earlier than their competitors.

Consider the Netflix example. The media company started to create original content to strengthen its competitive advantage over emerging competitors and lower its content costs in the longer run. And it used analytics to drive decisions on what original series and movies to make. *House of Cards*, for instance, was developed with predictions that a combination of Kevin Spacey as the lead cast, David Fincher as the director, and the political drama theme inspired by the original British television series would bring success.

Predictive analytics is also essential for selecting which product to offer from an existing portfolio of options. The predictive algorithm used is called recommendation systems, which suggest products to customers based on their history and preferences of similar customers. The propensity model estimates the likelihood of customers with specific profiles to buy when offered certain products. It enables marketers to provide customers with personalized value propositions. The longer the model works and the more customer response data it collects, the better the recommendations will be.

The recommendation engine is most commonly applied by retailers like Amazon or Walmart and digital services businesses such as YouTube or Tinder. But the application has made its way to other sectors as well. Any companies with a large customer base and a broad portfolio of products or content will find product recommendation engines valuable. The model will help the companies automate the process of matching the products and markets.

Moreover, the predictive recommendation model is most useful when products are bought and used together or in conjunction with one another. The modeling involves what is known as product affinity analysis. For instance, people who have bought shirts would probably be interested in buying matching trousers or shoes. And people who are reading a news article might want to read other articles written by the same reporter or learn more about the topic.

Predictive Brand Management

Predictive analytics can help marketers plan their brand and marketing communications activities, especially in the digital space. The main data analysis requirement includes building complete audience profiles and mapping the key ingredients of successful past campaigns. The analysis will be useful to envision which future campaigns are likely to succeed. Since machine learning is a constant endeavor, brand managers can continue to evaluate their campaigns and optimize where they may fall short.

When designing the advertising creative and developing content marketing, brand managers can utilize machine learning to gauge customer interests in various combinations of copies and visuals. Sentiment analysis in social media and third-party review websites can be used to understand how our customers feel about our brands and campaigns. They can also collect data on which digital campaigns drive the most clicks. Therefore, brand managers can create creatives and content that produce optimal outcomes, such as positive sentiments and high click-through rates.

Predictive analytics can also be a powerful tool to guide content distribution to the right audience. It works in two ways. Companies may design the branded content and then identify what customer segments will be the most effective to reach as well as when and where to engage them. Alternatively, companies can profile the customers and then predict which content will resonate with them most in every step in their journeys.

Customers might struggle to find the information they need in a large pool of content that brands broadcast. The prediction model can provide a solution by forecasting the right audience–content fit that produces the optimal outcome. Thus, marketers can break content clutter and perform a very targeted distribution to the intended audience.

In the digital space, businesses may easily track the customer journey across multiple websites and social media. Therefore, they can predict a customer's next move in their digital engagements. With this information, marketers can, for instance, design a dynamic website in which the content can change according to the audience. As customers browse through the website, the analytics engine predicts the next-best content that will gradually increase the level of interest and get the customer one step closer to purchase action.

Building Predictive Marketing Models

There are many techniques to create predictive marketing models from the simplest to the most sophisticated. Marketers will need the help of statisticians and data scientists to build and develop the models. Thus, they do not need to understand the statistical and mathematical models in depth. However, marketers need to understand the fundamental ideas behind a predictive model so that they can guide the technical teams to select data to use and which patterns to find. Moreover, marketers will also help interpret the model as well as the deployment of the predictions into operations.

Following are some of the most commonly used types of predictive modeling that marketers use for multiple purposes.

Regression Modeling for Simple Predictions

Regression modeling is the most fundamental yet useful tool for predictive analytics. The model assesses the relationship between independent variables (or explanatory data) and dependent variables (or response data). Dependent variables are the results or outcomes that marketers are trying to achieve, such as click and sales data. On the other hand, independent variables are the data that influence the results, such as campaign timing, advertising copy, or customer demographics.

In regression analysis, marketers look for statistical equations that explain the relationship between the dependent and independent variables. In other words, marketers are trying to understand which marketing actions have the most significant impact and drive the best outcomes for the business.

The relative simplicity of regression compared to other modeling techniques makes it the most popular. Regression analysis can be used for many predictive marketing applications, such as building the customer equity model, propensity model, churn detection model, and product affinity model.

In general, regression modeling is carried out in several steps.

1. **Gather the data for dependent and independent variables.**

   For regression analysis, datasets for both dependent and independent variables must be collected in unison and with sufficient sampling. For instance, marketers can investigate the impact of the digital banner color on the clickthrough rates by collecting a substantial enough sample of color and the resulting click data.

2. **Find the equation that explains the relationship between variables.**

   Using any statistical software, marketers can draw an equation that best fits the data. The most basic equation forms a straight line, which is known as a linear regression line. Another common one is the logistic regression, which uses a logistic function to model a binary dependent variable, such as buy or not buy and stay or churn. Thus, logistical regression is often used to predict the likelihood of an outcome, such as the probability to buy.

3. **Interpret the equation to reveal insights and check for accuracy.**

   Consider the following example. Let us say the best-fit equation is defined as follows:

   $$Y = a + bX_1 + cX_2 + dX_3 + e$$

   In the formula, Y is the dependent variable while X_1, X_2, and X_3 are the independent variables. The a is the intercept, which reflects the value of Y if there is no influence what-soever from independent variables. The b, c, and d are the coefficients of the independent variables, which indicate how much impact the variables have on the dependent variables. In the equation, we can also analyze the error term or residual (written as e). A regression formula always has errors, as the independent variables might not entirely explain the dependent variables. The larger the error term, the less accurate the equation is.

4. **Predict dependent variables given independent variables.**

Once the formula is established, marketers can predict the dependent variables based on the given independent variables. That way, marketers can envision the outcomes from a mix of marketing actions.

Collaborative Filtering for Recommendation Systems

The most popular technique to build recommendation systems is collaborative filtering. The underlying assumption is that people will like products similar to other products they have bought, or prefer products that are purchased by other people with the same preferences. It involves the collaboration of customers to rate products for the model to work, hence the name collaborative filtering. It also applies to not only products but also content, depending on what marketers aim to recommend to the customers.

In a nutshell, the collaborative filtering model works according to the following logical sequence:

1. **Collect preferences from a large customer base.**

To measure how much people prefer a product, marketers can create a community rating system where customers can rate a product either with a simple like/dislike (like in You-Tube) or a 5-star scoring (like in Amazon). Alternatively, marketers can use actions that reflect preference, such as reading an article, watching a video, and adding products to the wish list or shopping cart. Netflix, for instance, gauges preferences by movies that people watch over time.

2. **Cluster similar customers and products.**

Customers who have rated similar sets of products and have shown similar behaviors can be classified into the same cluster. The assumption is that they are part of the same psychographic (based on like/dislike) and behavioral (based on actions) segments. Alternatively, marketers can also cluster items that are similarly rated by a particular group of customers.

3. **Predict the rating that a customer will likely give a new product.**

Marketers can now predict ratings that customers will give to products they have not seen and rated based on ratings provided by like-minded customers. This predicted score is essential for marketers to offer the right products that the customers might like and will most likely act on in the future.

Neural Network for Complex Predictions

A neural network, as the name implies, is loosely modeled after how the biological neural network operates inside the human brain. It is one of the most popular machine learning tools that help businesses build sophisticated models for predictions. The neural network model learns from experience by processing a large number and a variety of past examples. Today, neural network models are readily accessible. Google, for instance, has made TensorFlow, its machine learning platform with neural networks, open-source software available to everyone.

Unlike a simple regression model, a neural network is considered as a black box because the inner workings are often hard for humans to interpret. In a way, it is similar to how humans sometimes cannot explain the way they make decisions based on the information at hand. However, it is also suitable to build models from unstructured data where the data scientists and business teams are unable to determine the best algorithm to use.

In lay terms, the following steps explain how a neural network operates:

1. **Load two sets of data: the input and the output.**

   A neural network model consists of an input layer, output layers, and hidden layers in between. Similar to how we build a regression model, the independent variables are loaded into the input layer while the dependent variables go into the output layer. The difference, however, is in the hidden layers, which essentially contain the black-box algorithms.

2. **Let the neural networks discover connections between the data.**

   A neural network is capable of connecting the data to derive a function or a predictive model. The way it works is similar to how human brains connect the dots based on our lifelong learning. The neural network will discover all kinds of patterns and relationships between each data set: correlations, associations, dependencies, and causalities. Some of these connections may be previously unknown and hidden.

3. **Use the resulting model in the hidden layers to predict output.**

   The functions derived from example data can be used to predict the output from a new given input. And when the actual output is loaded back to the neural network, the machine learns from its inaccuracy and refines the hidden layers over time. Thus, it is called machine learning. Although it does not reveal real-world insights due to its complexity, the neural network model coming from continuous machine learning can be very accurate in its predictions.

The choice of predictive models depends on the problem at hand. When the problem is structured and easy to grasp, regression modeling suffices. But when the issue involves unknown factors or algorithms, machine learning methods such as neural networks will work best. Marketers can also use more than one model to find the best fit with the data that they have (see Figure 9.2).

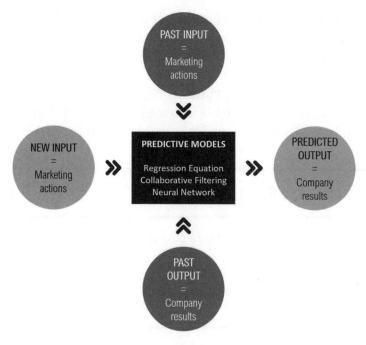

FIGURE 9.2   How Predictive Marketing Works

Summary: Anticipating Market Demand with Proactive Action

Data-driven marketers can stay ahead of the curve by predicting the outcomes of every marketing action. In customer management, predictive analytics can help companies estimate the value of their potential customers before onboarding and determine how much investment to get and grow them.

In product management, marketers can envision the sales results of a pre-launch product prototype and determine which product line to upsell and cross-sell from an extensive portfolio. And finally, predictive modeling can enable brand managers to analyze their customer sentiments and decide how to build their brands in the given context.

There are several popular techniques of predictive marketing modeling, which include regression analysis, collaborative filtering, and neural networks. Machine learning or artificial intelligence might be utilized to build predictive models. Thus, most marketers will need the technical help of statisticians and data scientists. But marketers must have a strategic understanding of how the models work and how to draw insights from them.

REFLECTION QUESTIONS

- Has your organization leveraged predictive analytics for marketing? Explore some new applications of predictive marketing.
- How will you deploy predictive marketing and integrate it into operations? How will the predictive models be socialized around the organization?

CHAPTER 10

Contextual Marketing

Making a Personalized Sense-and-Respond Experience

In 2019, Walgreens began testing smart coolers that combine cameras, sensors, and digital screen doors to display the products inside as well as a personalized advertisement to shoppers. While the technology does not recognize faces and store identities for privacy reasons, it does predict shoppers' age and gender. The fridge uses facial detection to deduce the demographic and emotions of a shopper approaching the cooler door. It also utilizes eye-tracking and motion sensors to gauge the shopper's interest.

By combining these insights with external information such as the weather or local events, the AI engine can select specific products and promotions to push on the screens. The refrigerator also tracks what the shopper picks and recommends another matching item once the door is closed. As you might expect, it collects lots of data about shopper behaviors and which product packaging or campaign works.

The smart cooler system—provided by Cooler Screens—has brought multiple advantages. Walgreens has seen growth in traffic and purchases in stores that have it installed. The chain also gets additional revenue from placed ads. Moreover, the technology allows quick changes in prices and promotions for experimentation purposes. It enables brands to monitor stocks as well as get feedback on their newest campaigns.

This sort of dynamic advertising and contextual content model is not new in the digital marketing space. Brands have been using it to push tailored ads based on customers' web browsing history. With smart coolers, the model is brought to the retail space, essentially bridging the physical and digital worlds. Today, marketers can perform contextual marketing in an automated fashion with the help of the next tech.

Indeed, the long-term goal of the next tech, such as the Internet of Things (IoT) and artificial intelligence (AI), is to replicate human situational awareness. Well-versed marketers can offer the right products to the right customers at the right moment and in the right place. Seasoned salespeople who have built long-term relationships know their customers deeply and serve each one with a tailored approach. The mission is to deliver this contextual experience at scale with the help of IoT and AI.

Building Smart Sensing Infrastructure

Humans develop situational awareness by scanning the environment for sensory cues. We can tell other people's emotions by looking at their facial expressions and gestures. We know if people are annoyed or if they are happy with us. For computers to do the same, it requires a variety of sensors to collect all the cues for AI to process.

Using Proximity Sensors for Contextual Response at the Point of Sale

The first step to create AI-powered contextual marketing is to set up a connected ecosystem of sensors and devices, especially at the point of sale (POS). One of the most popular sensors used at the POS is a beacon—a Bluetooth low-energy transmitter that communicates with nearby devices. With multiple beacons set up in any physical establishment, marketers can pinpoint customer locations as well as track movement. The sensors can also help marketers send personalized content to the connected devices, for instance, in the form of push notifications.

Companies need to determine which specific condition will trigger the sensors to perform location-based actions. The best contextual trigger is the presence of a customer. The challenge, however, is to recognize the identity or the profile of the customer to ensure that the response is truly personalized. For instance, a customer with the right age and gender profile approaching a retail store aisle might be an excellent prompt to send customized discount offers. Environmental variables, such as the weather, can also be a contextual trigger. When it is hot outside is perhaps the best time to promote cold drinks (see Figure 10.1).

To make it work, marketers need to leverage the device that is always in the customer's possession as a proxy for the where-abouts. A smartphone is one alternative. Smartphones have become a very personal device that customers always keep close. The device is replacing a wallet, a key, and a camera for a lot of people. Most importantly, smartphones are abundant with sensors and are always connected either through Bluetooth or a mobile network. That way, mobile phones can connect and communicate with the sensors.

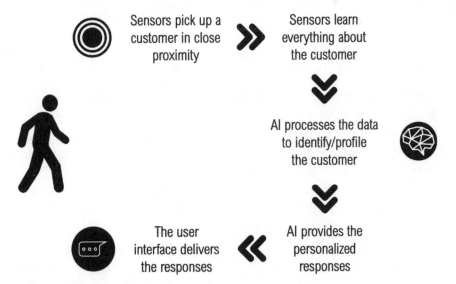

FIGURE 10.1   Contextual Marketing Mechanism

When a customer with the right mobile app is nearby, a beacon or a proximity sensor reaches out to the customer. Let us say, for example, the customer has installed an app for a retailer and logged into the app with their personal information. Once triggered by the proximity of the mobile phone, the beacon can send a customized message as an app notification.

Imagine if beacons are installed in every aisle in retail stores, theme parks, malls, hotels, casinos, or any other physical establishments. Companies can utilize customer mobile phones as navigation tools, providing information and promotion as customers walk through the physical locations. It creates a highly contextual journey for the customers. Macy's, Target, CVS, and other major retailers are using beacon technology for this particular purpose.

The role of smartphones can be replaced with wearable devices—and even implantable ones in the future. Smartphone manufacturers have been aggressively offering smartwatches, earbuds, and fitness bands, which can potentially be an even more personal device to customers. Although not yet as popular as smartphones, certain wearables are still promising as they also contain customer micro-movement and health information. Disney and the Mayo Clinic, for example, use RFID bands to track and analyze people's location and movement.

Utilizing Biometrics to Trigger Personalized Actions

Another popular contextual trigger is the customers themselves. Without any personal devices, customers can trigger location-based actions just by showing their faces. A growing technology, facial recognition enables companies not only to estimate the demographic profiles but also to identify individual persons once they are recorded in the database. It allows marketers to deliver the right contextual response to the right person.

Similar to Walgreens and its smart coolers, Tesco began installing face detection technology at its petrol stations in the United Kingdom. The camera will capture a driver's face, and an AI engine will predict the age and gender. The driver will get targeted ads specifically for the demographic profile while they are waiting for the gas tank to be refueled.

Bestore, a snack food chain in China, utilizes Alibaba's facial recognition database to scan and identify people who give their consent. The technology lets the store attendants see what snack customers like—based on Alibaba data—the moment they enter the shop. That way, the attendants can offer the right product for each shopper. The facial recognition technology is not only useful for customer identification. The retail chain also uses Alipay's "Smile to Pay" facial recognition payment system for store checkout.

Facial recognition technology is now capable of detecting people's feelings, too. AI algorithms can infer emotions by analyzing human facial expressions in images, recorded videos, and live cameras. The feature is beneficial for marketers to understand how customers respond to their products and campaigns without the presence of a human observer.

Thus, emotion detection is used for product concept and ad testing in online interviews and focus groups. Respondents who share access to their webcams are asked to watch a picture or a video and have their facial reactions analyzed. For instance, Kellogg's used facial expression analysis from Affectiva for developing ads for Crunchy Nut. The company tracks the viewer's amusement and engagement when watching the commercials during the first viewing and repetition.

Disney experimented with emotion detection by installing cameras in cinemas showing its movies. Tracking millions of facial expressions throughout the film, Disney can learn how much moviegoers enjoy every scene. It is useful to improve filmmaking for future projects.

Due to its real-time analysis, the same technology can be utilized to provide responsive content according to the audience's reactions. The obvious use case will be for dynamic ads on out-of-home (OOH) billboards. Ocean Outdoor, an outdoor advertising company, installed billboards with cameras that detect audience mood, age, and gender to deliver targeted ads in the United Kingdom.

Another use case in development is for car drivers. A few automakers began testing facial recognition technology to enhance the experience. Upon recognizing the car owner's face, a car can automatically open, start, and even play the owner's favorite playlist. And when the technology detects that the driver's face looks tired, it can recommend that the driver take a rest.

A related technology is an eye-tracking sensor. With this technology, companies can understand where a viewer focuses attention based on eye movements, for example, when seeing an ad or a video. Marketers can essentially create a heatmap and learn which specific areas in the ad create more excitement and engagement. Palace Resorts utilized eye tracking in its marketing campaign. The hospitality company creates a microsite where visitors can take a video quiz and give their consent for the use of eye-tracking technology via webcams. Visitors will be asked to choose from a pair of videos with a combination of various holiday elements. Based on the direction of their gaze, the site will recommend one of the company's resorts that best fits the interests of the visitor.

Voice is another way to recognize humans and trigger contextual actions. AI can analyze the properties of vocal speech—speed, brief pauses, and tones—and discover embedded emotions. The health insurance company Humana uses voice analysis from Cogito in its call centers to understand a caller's feelings and recommend a conversational technique to the call center agent. When the caller sounds annoyed, for example, the AI engine will give alerts to the agent to change approach. It is essentially coaching the agents to build a better connection with the callers in real time.

British Airways also experiments with understanding its passengers' mood onboard the aircraft. It launched the "happiness blanket," which can change color based on a passenger's state of mind. The blanket came with a headband that monitors brain waves and determines if a passenger is anxious or relaxed. The experiment helped the airline understand changes in mood across the customer journey: when watching in-flight entertainment, during meal service, or when sleeping. Most importantly, the technology allows flight attendants to quickly identify which passengers are unhappy and make them feel more comfortable.

Mood detection from facial expressions, eye movements, voice, and neuro-signals is not yet mainstream in marketing applications. But it will be the key to the future of contextual marketing. It is critical to understand the customer's state of mind, aside from their basic demographic profiles.

Creating a Direct Channel to Customer Premises

IoT penetrates customer homes, too. Everything from security systems to home entertainment to household appliances is connected to the Internet. The rise of smart homes provides a channel for marketers to promote products and services directly to where customers live. It helps marketing move ever closer to the point of consumption.

One of the growing channels for marketers in customer homes is the smart speakers such as Amazon Echo, Google Nest, and Apple HomePod. Each is powered by intelligent voice assistants: Alexa, Google Assistant, and Siri. These smart speakers essentially act as voice-activated search engines, to which customers ask questions and look for information. Like search engines, they will become more intelligent as they learn more about their owners' habits and behaviors through numerous inquiries. Therefore, it potentially can be a powerful contextual marketing channel.

Marketing on these smart speaker systems is still in the early stages as direct advertising is not currently available on any of the platforms. However, many workarounds are possible. For instance, Amazon Echo allows users to train Alexa with specific skills to make it more useful. Companies like P&G and Campbell's are publishing skills related to their products. For the Tide brand, P&G created an Alexa skill that answers hundreds of questions about laundry. Campbell's released an Alexa skill that provides answers to recipe inquiries. As customers ask these questions and get answers, brands get increased awareness and higher intention-to-buy.

Most smart appliances also provide a screen space for promotion. Samsung's Family Hub—a refrigerator with a touchscreen display—allows shoppers to build a shopping list and order groceries directly from the Instacart app. The smart fridge also enables customers to request an Uber ride or order food from GrubHub. The intelligent appliance ecosystem empowers marketers to be instantly available with the right products and services the moment customers need them the most.

More advanced utilization of connected devices at home is for 3D printing. The technology is still in infancy because it is considered expensive and complicated. But companies are exploring ways to bring it to mainstream usage. Hershey and 3D Systems introduced CocoJet's 3D chocolate printer in 2014. With CocoJet, users can print chocolate of various shapes and put a personalized message on a chocolate bar. This sort of technology brings the point of production closer to the point of consumption.

Although more popular in the business-to-customer (B2C), contextual marketing is very much applicable in the business-to-business (B2B) settings. Since B2B companies do not necessarily have retail outlets, the IoT sensors are installed on their products at customer premises. Heavy equipment manufacturers, for example, can install sensors in the machinery that they sell to monitor performance. The companies can then provide the contextual data to their customers for preventive maintenance regularly and eventually save costs.

Delivering Three Levels of Personalized Experience

Customization and personalization in the digital world are straightforward. Marketers use digital information about the customers to deliver dynamic content that fits the profile. In the physical space, customization and personalization used to rely heavily on the human touch. With the IoT and AI infrastructure in place, companies can bring the digital capability to tailor marketing action into the physical world without too much human intervention.

Custom-made marketing can be delivered at three levels. The first level is informative marketing. At this level, marketers provide the right offer: marketing communication message, product selection, or price promotion. The second level is interactive marketing, where marketers create a channel of two-way communication interface and intelligently interact with the customers. The ultimate level is immersive marketing, at which marketers engage customers deeply in sensory experiences.

Level 1: Personalized Information

Location-based marketing, in its narrow application, is the most common type of informative marketing. It leverages one of the most valuable metadata: the geolocation. The data are typically captured via the global positioning system (GPS) of customer smartphones. For indoor use, the geolocation data can be further enhanced with the use of proximity sensors or beacons.

With the data, marketers usually perform geofencing marketing practice, which is creating a virtual perimeter around a specific point of interest (such as a retail store, airport, office, and school) and broadcasting targeted messages to the audience within the perimeter. All major social media advertising platforms, such as Facebook and Google, provide geofencing capabilities. It means that campaigns can be isolated to a specific area.

Companies can use geofencing to drive traffic to their stores from nearby locations or competitors' locations with promotional offers. Companies like Sephora, Burger King, and Whole Foods use location-based marketing. Burger King, for example, created a geofence around more than 14,000 McDonald's locations as well as more than 7,000 outlets of their own across the United States in its Whopper Detour campaign. Users of Burger King's mobile app could order a Whopper for a penny, but only if they are near a McDonald's outlet. Once the order is placed, the users are directed to move from the McDonald's outlet to a nearby Burger King to get their Whoppers.

Level 2: Customized Interaction

The contextual marketing in its interactive format is multilayered. Customers do not receive a direct call to purchase in the location-based offers. Instead, they are given a chance to respond to the location-based message they receive, and based on the response, companies send another message, essentially creating a dialogue. With this approach, companies can trigger customers to move to the next step in the customer journey, from awareness to action, by giving them the right incentives or the right offer. The benefit of this approach is that customers will be more compelled to buy the products, having gone through several interactions in a more comprehensive journey.

To make contextual marketing more interactive, companies can use the principles of gamification. Shopkick, a shopping reward app, collaborates with American Eagle and many other retailers to provide shoppers incentives to move forward in their path-to-purchase. The app incentivizes people every step of the way. Shoppers get rewards by walking into the store, scanning a barcode to learn more about a product, and trying on clothes in fitting rooms.

Consider another example from Sephora. The company makes contextual marketing more interactive by allowing customers to follow up on their location-based offers with in-store consultation. The process starts when customers try Sephora Virtual Artist—an augmented reality tool that allows them to see how makeup products work on their faces, available online and in-store at a kiosk. When they are nearby a store, they will be reminded to visit and book an in-store consultation, making it more likely for the customers to buy the products.

Level 3: Total Immersion

The ultimate level of personalization is when marketers can provide total immersion in the physical space with the help of sensors and other technologies, such as augmented reality or robotics. The idea is to surround customers with digital experience while they are in brick-and-mortar stores.

Big box retailers, for instance, use geolocation data and augmented reality to provide immersive in-store navigation. Take an example from Lowe's mobile app. Shoppers can create a shopping list inside the mobile app and add the items that they want to purchase on the list. Once they are done, shoppers can activate the augmented reality feature, and a yellow-colored path will appear onscreen on the ground in front of them. The route takes customers to the items on the list in the shortest distance possible.

Fashion brands, such as Ralph Lauren, are using the smart fitting room to provide immersive digital experience in the physical world. Customers can bring fashion items that they like to the fitting room and interact with a digital mirror. With RFID technology, all of the pieces brought to the fitting room are instantly shown onscreen. Customers can choose different sizes and colors, and store attendants will bring the items to the fitting room and even recommend particular styles.

The objective of immersive, contextual marketing is to blur the borders between the physical and digital worlds so that customers feel a seamless omnichannel experience. That way we can combine the personalization power of digital technology and the experiential nature of brick-and-mortar establishments.

Summary: Making a Personalized Sense-and-Respond Experience

IoT and AI make a powerful combination in the goal to create a contextual marketing experience in the brick-and-mortar world. The dynamic marketing based on customer data is native to the digital media. Digital marketers can easily tailor marketing offers in an automated fashion. The application of contextual marketing in the physical space in the past often depended on the ability of frontline staff to read their customers. With the help of IoT and AI, that is no longer the case.

The most critical element to establish AI-powered contextual marketing is to build a connected ecosystem of sensors

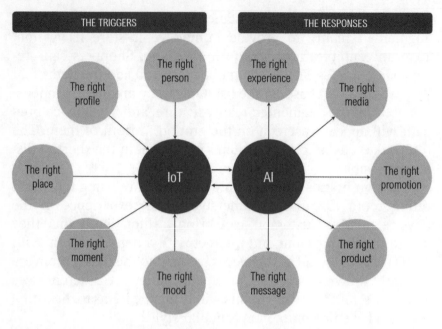

FIGURE 10.2   The Triggers and Responses in Contextual Marketing

and devices, either in the POS or on customer premises. Once the infrastructure is in place, marketers will only need to define the triggers and responding actions. When the right person with the right profile is nearby the sensors, marketers can learn more about the person and offer the right products with the right message. Marketers can also interact with and even develop an immersive customer experience for that person (see Figure 10.2).

REFLECTION QUESTIONS

- Think about how you would leverage contextual marketing technology in your organization. What are some of the opportunities to apply a combination of IoT and AI?
- Explore ways for you to personalize your marketing approach based on your real-time understanding of the customers.

CHAPTER 11

Augmented Marketing

Delivering Tech-Empowered Human Interaction

One of the major headlines in the late 1990s was the chess games between IBM's Deep Blue and Grandmaster Garry Kasparov as the quintessential man-versus-machine matchup. In 1997, the supercomputer eventually became the first machine to beat a reigning world champion in a chess game. Although a year prior, Kasparov had won the first match, the defeat became all the buzz in the chess world and beyond.

Many experts attributed the win as a sign of the machine's superior intelligence. Deep Blue could process 200 million positions per second at the time, much faster than any human could. Kasparov himself admitted his uncertainty about Deep Blue's capability during the game. With a human opponent, it was more predictable as he could read their facial expression and body language.

In the aftermath, many chess players, including Kasparov, were curious whether they could augment their playing ability with a computer on their side. It led to a form of competition known as the advanced or freestyle chess, in which human players can consult with machines before deciding their every move. A breakthrough insight was revealed in 2005, where in a tournament with grandmasters and supercomputers participating, the winner turned out to be two amateur chess players, Steven Cramton and Zackary Stephen, assisted by three regular computers (Team ZackS).

Leading to the final, several grandmasters with help from computers had defeated most supercomputer competitors. The only exception was Team ZackS, who had also defeated some supercomputers along the way. In the final, Team ZackS won against a team of grandmasters and the supporting computers. The amateur players had taught their machines better than any grandmaster or any self-learning computer.

The story is often cited as proof that human–machine collaboration is always better than either a human expert or a powerful machine. The key is to find the best symbiosis between the two. Today, supercomputers are nowhere near replicating the highly nuanced human intelligence, and the dream of artificial general intelligence (AGI) is still far from being realized (see Chapter 6). But computers have been excellent at taking over specific functions from humans. Instead of building machines that are capable of doing everything, technologists focus on developing several narrow AI applications where machines outperform humans.

Knowing precisely what and how to teach computers will enable human coaches to realize their full potential. This premise leads to a technology development movement known as intelligence amplification (IA). As opposed to artificial intelligence (AI), which aims to replicate human intelligence, IA seeks to augment human intelligence with technology. In IA, humans remain the ones making decisions, albeit supported by robust computational analysis.

In marketing, the application of IA makes perfect sense in areas where humans are still dominant and computers can only become the support systems. Thus, augmented marketing focuses on marketing activities that heavily involve human-to-human interfaces, such as selling and customer service. In these human resources–intensive jobs, the role of technology is to increase productivity by taking over low-value tasks and helping humans make smarter decisions.

Building Tiered Customer Interfaces

Customer interface—the way customers communicate with companies—is a big part of the customer experience. In industries such as hospitality, healthcare, professional services, and even high-tech, some customer interfaces are mainly fronted by humans. The concierges, nurses, consultants, and key account managers are critical resources in their fields, and machines are not a match for their abilities to deliver the right experience. But it takes years to recruit and develop the competencies of these people before they can perform their best. The circumstance makes companies challenging to scale, essentially creating a limit to growth.

Augmented marketing offers a solution to this problem. Digital interfaces will provide new alternative ways for customers to interact with brands and companies. Gartner estimates that 72% of customer interactions will involve emerging technologies such as AI, chatbot, and mobile messaging by 2022. Although a digital interface cannot wholly replace human-to-human interaction, it can make the scarce human resources work faster and smarter.

The rise of Generation Y and Generation Z will further fuel this need for augmented marketing (see Chapter 2). These two generations see the Internet as an indispensable part of their lives and technology as an extension of themselves. In fact, they see no borders between the physical and digital worlds. They call it the "phygital" world. The need for speed and on-demand delivery will make way for digital interfaces.

Augmented marketing starts with a clear definition of how technologies can add value to frontline operations. One way to improve productivity is to create a tiered interface system. Mixing the digital and human interfaces within a structured pyramid allows businesses to scale up. Companies can free human resources to work on worthwhile tasks.

Tiered Sales Interfaces

In the selling process, the most common customer interface tiering is based on the customer lifecycle across the sales funnel. B2B companies can capture and nurture early leads via a digital interface while pursuing qualified leads and hot prospects with a team of salespeople. With this approach, businesses can have a broader reach with lead generation. At the same time, they can refocus the sales force efforts into closing the deals. This arrangement is optimal since the final step in the sales funnels usually requires strong communication and negotiation skills.

Retail businesses can also leverage tiered sales interfaces with omnichannel presence. Digital channels are used to build awareness, create attraction, and encourage trials. Customers can browse through a catalog of products on the website or mobile app and select what they like. Companies like Sephora and IKEA use augmented reality (AR) to enable potential buyers to "try on" the product digitally. That way, when customers come to the brick-and-mortar outlet, the interest has built up and it is easier for store attendants to sell.

The division of labor between human and machine in the sales process is based on activity specialization across the funnel. This hybrid model uses various sales channels from those with the lowest cost to the most expensive ones. Each channel plays a specific role that drives prospects from the top to the bottom of the funnel (see Figure 11.1).

Several steps are required to design the tiered interface that creates the best symbiosis between people and computers:

1. **Determine the steps in the sales process.**

   A typical sales process is funnel-like, which means that the sales team converts a large pool of leads to a smaller number

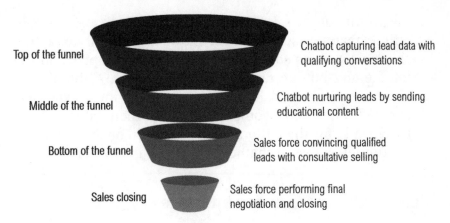

Top of the funnel — Chatbot capturing lead data with qualifying conversations

Middle of the funnel — Chatbot nurturing leads by sending educational content

Bottom of the funnel — Sales force convincing qualified leads with consultative selling

Sales closing — Sales force performing final negotiation and closing

FIGURE 11.1   Example of Augmented Marketing in Tiered Sales Interface

of customers step-by-step. The quality of the sales process will show in the conversion rates across the funnel. The top of the funnel process (ToFu) includes building awareness, generating leads, qualifying leads, and capturing lead data. The middle of the funnel (MoFu) usually involves nurturing the leads to make them hot prospects. Finally, the bottom of the funnel (BoFu) process includes meeting and convincing the leads as well as negotiation and sales closing.

2. **Build a list of possible sales interfaces.**

In the past, the sales process relied a lot on trade shows and email marketing to build awareness and generate leads. To nurture the leads and close them, companies relied on telesales and direct salesforce. With advanced technologies, many alternative interfaces emerge. Digital marketing now has broad enough reach for an awareness campaign. Businesses can use various alternative channels to process the leads, such as with a self-service website, an AR-enabled mobile app, an AI-enabled chatbot, and live chat—all at a lower cost.

3. **Match the funnel activity with the best interface option.**

To determine which interface plays which role in the process, it is not always only about cutting costs. Companies need to balance efficiency and effectiveness. Depending on the profiles of the sales leads, marketers can choose between offline channels such as trade shows and digital marketing channels such as social media. Similar logic applies in the middle and bottom of the funnel processes. Although the most effective, the salesforce remains the most expensive channel. Thus, most companies reserve their valuable time specifically for the bottom of the funnel. For the middle of the funnel, AI-based chatbot can replace the role of telesales.

Tiered Customer Service Interfaces

In the customer service process—in other words, when dealing with existing customers—the most common basis for customer tiering is the customer lifetime value (CLV) or customer loyalty status.

The CLV is a projected net income generated from each customer based on the estimated length of tenure. Customers with low CLV or status only have access to the digital interface, hence the low cost-to-serve. On the other hand, customers with high CLV have the privilege to interact with high-cost human assistants. The service quality tiering provides the incentive for customers to climb up the ladder by making a bigger purchase or committing their loyalty to specific brands.

The rich information that can be found on the Internet makes people search for solutions themselves when stumbling into a problem with products and services. Many companies facilitate the self-service trend by providing searchable online resources for their customers. Many also develop support forums or communities where customers can ask one another about their problems. In this social technology application, the volunteers who helped others are rewarded with gamification badges. A longtime best practice for tech companies, the approach is now adopted by businesses in other industries. With a strong knowledge base and support forums, companies can anticipate customer issues, and customers can avoid the unnecessary hassle of contacting customer service.

The knowledge bases from online resources and forums become a big structured data that companies feed to their machine learning algorithms. Instead of searching for answers in support pages or communities, customers can now just ask AI for solutions. The automated customer service interface may be a chatbot or a virtual assistant. It gives customers not only convenience but also the instant solutions that they want. Similarly, scripts and histories from call centers and live chats can now be transferred to the AI engine, essentially providing hassle-free options for customers having basic, frequently asked questions.

Businesses need to take several steps to develop tiered customer support with a solid symbiosis between humans and machines:

1. **Build a knowledge base of frequently asked questions.**

   Businesses learn from past histories that most customer inquiries are basic and repetitive. It is inefficient to use customer service reps to respond to these questions. Thus, the first thing that companies must do is compile these questions into a library of information that is easily accessible. A good structure and categorization will help customers navigate through the knowledge base. Companies should use storyboards that utilize actual customer stories—real situations and scenarios that customers face. Moreover, a good knowledge base must have a search function. And finally, it should also be continuously updated with new information.

2. **Determine customer tiering model.**

   With analytics, businesses can quickly analyze a large volume of transactions into individual customer records. Companies need to simply determine a set of criteria to evaluate the value of each customer to them. Usually, the tiering involves both financial (revenue, profitability) and nonfinancial measures (share of wallet, tenure, strategic importance). Based on the criteria, companies can group customers into levels. The tiering is dynamic; there must be a mechanism for customers to move up and down. When the tiering is well defined, it is straightforward to determine the cost-to-serve budgets for each tier. The budgets will determine which customer support options each customer can access.

3. Create multitier customer support options.

Companies can leverage the knowledge base for several customer service channels. The first is to create a self-service option by putting the knowledge base on the website. When the knowledge base has flowing storyboards, it can be easily transferred to both the chatbots and virtual assistant (e.g. Alexa skills) platforms. When customers fail to get answers having gone through these machine interfaces, companies should provide an option to escalate to human-to-human interfaces. Forums and communities are great ways to empower customers. But ultimately, customer service reps must be ready to give answers when nobody else can, either via email, live chat, or phone call. Companies should not provide all these options to everyone. Low-tier customers will typically get access to self-service options (online resources and forums) while high-tier customers will get all types of access depending on their preferences (see Figure 11.2).

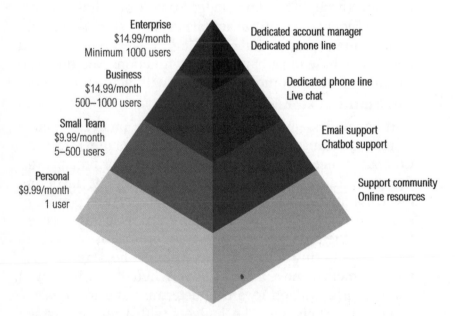

FIGURE 11.2 Example of Augmented Marketing in Tiered Customer Service Interface

Providing Digital Tools for Frontliners

Augmented marketing is not only about the division of labor. Digital tools can empower frontline employees who have direct interactions with customers. Today, despite all the buzz surrounding e-commerce and online shopping, the majority of retail sales still happen in brick-and-mortar stores. Most customers are still webrooming—search online and shop offline. Thus, when well-informed customers who have spent hours researching products online eventually come to the store, they expect equally knowledgeable frontline staff to interact with them.

A similar trend happens in the services industry, too. Customers are accustomed to reading reviews before coming to hotels, professional services firms, or education institutions to explore further. These smarter customers have high expectations, and that makes the job of frontline employees more challenging.

Frontline personnel are crucially important, especially in high-contact environments such as the retail and services sectors. Even in low-contact industries, frontline staff often become the last line of defense in terms of service recoveries. They can often become the source of differentiation and the face of the brands. It is vital to empower employees with the right knowledge that companies have on their customers. Customer-facing employees are the most important medium to educate the customers on the things that are difficult to convey through other means.

With a wealth of insights, frontline staff can be more productive. They can focus on sales conversion, cross-selling, and upselling rather than making smart guesses about the customers. Transaction histories and AI-generated product recommendations are some of the information that will help employees understand what to offer the customers. Being able to anticipate customer needs is essential for frontline work. Equally important is to be able to provide personalized interactions and build relationships as if they have known the customers for a long time.

Digital tools in the brick-and-mortar stores also help reduce friction for companies aiming to provide omnichannel experience. Consider the Sephora Digital Makeover Guide. A customer can book an appointment with a makeup artist. Once in-store, the customer can browse the online lookbook for a makeover inspiration. The artist uses a small scanner called Color IQ to capture the skin tone to determine the perfect shade for the customer. With the information from the lookbook and Color IQ, the artist can look for and scan products that fit the customer profile. Once the makeover is completed, the artist can email the customer the list of steps and products that have been used—useful for a repeat purchase.

Businesses need to build not only a digital interface for the customers but also a matching one for the employees. The delivery of customer information can be made via either mobile devices or wearables. Hotels, for instance, may allow customers to make requests via in-room tablets or their smartphones, and those requests can reach the housekeeping, kitchen, or concierge directly or via a connecting chatbot. It facilitates faster response and hence creates a better customer experience.

There are several steps for companies to provide the right digital tools to support frontline employees:

1. **Understand employee frustration points.**

   The biggest mistake companies make in implementing digital tools in frontline operations is to focus on the technology and not the reason for implementing it. Understanding employee experience (EX) is equally essential as understanding customer experience (CX). Thus, the first step is to map the employee experience journey as complementary information to the customer experience map. Frontline work is both difficult and stressful. But it also holds a lot of insight. Businesses need to listen to the voice of customer-facing employees and pinpoint their frustrations. Similar to customers, employees are usually frustrated with inefficiencies—activities that are time-consuming for them—and potential service failures—inability to give customers what they want, which leads to complaints.

2. **Identify how technology can be a solution.**

   Once the frustration points have been identified, companies need to find technology solutions that work. Most of the time, companies focus on the solutions that can be integrated into the entire information technology system. But the key to making the right selection, however, is to involve employees in the process. Tests need to be carried out with employee support. It will help companies anticipate potential issues in the execution early on and increase buy-in. Understanding how frontline workers use technology is critical, too. Companies need to choose the right hardware. Smartphones and tablets are standard digital tools for some tasks. But for other roles that require hands-free applications, wearables might make more sense.

3. **Focus on change management.**

   Unlike other elements of Marketing 5.0, augmented marketing requires close collaboration between frontline employees and technology enablers. The biggest challenge, especially for businesses with a large number of frontline workers, is the resistance to change. Not all customers are tech-savvy; likewise, not all employees are digital-ready. Not everyone is comfortable being augmented by technology. Training to upgrade digital skills is critical to success. But the learning is not only about the skills but also the digital mindset. Monitoring execution hurdles and fixing them is also something that businesses must pay attention to in the rollout.

Summary: Delivering Tech-Empowered Human Interaction

One of the areas where human–machine symbiosis provides the best outcome is in the customer interface. For basic and straightforward inquiries, digital interfaces suffice. But for more consultative interactions, computers have yet to outperform human-to-human interface. Thus, a division of labor within a tiered structure makes sense.

In the sales process, the top and middle of the funnel can be delegated to machines while the bottom one is carried out by the salesforce. In customer service, the digital and self-service interface is used to serve the mass of customers while the customer support reps are reserved for the most valuable customers. Businesses should utilize narrow artificial intelligence to ensure the quality of digital interactions.

Augmented marketing is also about empowering frontline employees with digital technologies. Smart and always-on customers must be matched by well-informed employees. Making data-driven insights available at the point of interaction allows employees to tailor their approach to every customer. A two-way interface between customers and employees also reduces friction and ultimately improves customer experience.

REFLECTION QUESTIONS

- Explore areas where you can improve the productivity of your frontline sales and customer service staff. What are some tasks that can be taken over by a computer system?
- How can you empower your frontline staff to make better decisions? For instance, how can your salespeople use customer targeting data to improve the sales conversion rate?

CHAPTER 12

Agile Marketing

Executing Operations at Pace and Scale

Zara has been one of the most successful fast-fashion brands in the last decade. Unlike traditional apparel companies that rely on longer seasonal trends, Inditex—the owner of Zara brand—is banking on quick turnaround time with more than 10,000 different designs per year. Inditex can bring the latest trends from the catwalk to the storefront in only a couple of weeks. Behind this extraordinary speed is an agile design and supply chain.

The company monitors trends of celebrity apparel and fashion shows around the world. It also analyzes the sales of each stock keeping unit (SKU) at the store level to determine which items have strong demand in real time, using radio-frequency identification (RFID) tracking. The market insights dictate decentralized teams of designers on which items to create. The sourcing is often done concurrently with the design process, making the process a lot quicker. Zara products are also made in small batches, ensuring high inventory turnover while allowing the brand to test market acceptance before committing to more production volume.

Zara's go-to-market practice is an example of agile marketing. Real-time analytics, decentralized quick response teams, flexible product platforms, concurrent processes, and rapid experimentation are all hallmarks of an agile organization. With this model, the brand has changed the way people buy clothes and accessories.

But fast-fashion retailing is a polarizing business. Despite having a strong fan base, the retailers also draw criticism, especially for their enormous waste and unfair labor practices. An agile organization must quickly sense and respond to market sentiments. Hence, Zara announced its support toward the circular economy—continuous use of materials through reuse and recycle. Zara also pledges that all of its clothing products will be made from sustainable materials by 2025.

The biggest test for Zara's agility is how the company will operate in the post-pandemic world. Zara typically uses its stores as e-commerce fulfillment centers. With stores temporarily closed during lockdowns and 1,200 stores to be permanently shut down globally, the plan needs readjustment. Integration between online and brick-and-mortar businesses will be the key for the brand in the next decade.

Why Agile Marketing?

A short product lifecycle characterizes the high-tech industry. The players are competing to be the first to market and capture maximum value before the technology becomes obsolete. Companies need to monitor and respond to new trends and changing customer behaviors. New product iterations are rapid since the window in which to profit from the products is limited. Hence, high-tech companies are the first to adopt agile marketing.

In the fast-paced digital world, many other industries— apparel, consumer packaged goods, consumer electronics, and automotive—are experiencing shortened product lifecycles to varying degrees. In these industries, customer preferences toward products are quickly changing, driven by new proliferating offerings. Even customer experience has an expiry date. The once-compelling experience can become outdated as soon as everyone else catches up and supersedes it.

The always-connected digital environment leads to these rapidly changing preferences. The customer experience, which used to be very private, can be broadcast to everyone else via social media, lessening its *wow* factor whenever businesses attempt to replicate it the second time. Always-on customers also demand always-on brands that cater to their needs 24/7. Everything is on-demand, or as Tom March called it, the new WWW (whatever, whenever, wherever). Consequently, companies must continually monitor and act on the ongoing trends and conversations at a faster rate.

Traditional, pre-planned go-to-market strategies are no longer effective. In an era of full of volatility, uncertainty, complexity, and ambiguity (VUCA), businesses can no longer make long-term plans without making numerous adjustments along the way. In fact, most long-term plans are already outdated by the time the milestones are reached.

Businesses need to match the speed of customer shifts and outpace the competition at the same time. Agility is the new name of the game. Operational stability used to be the only critical success factor for companies to scale up and grow. Although still vital, it must also be complemented by agile teams that become the catalysts for new growth engines. Agile marketing is the final piece of the puzzle for companies to implement Marketing 5.0. The discipline suits the fast-paced and unpredictable business landscape that they are facing.

Setting Up Agile Marketing

Agile marketing requires a certain kind of mindset that traditional companies lack. By default, startup companies already have agile mentalities due to their scarce resources. These companies need to make things happen quickly before their shoestring budget runs out. Large companies, however, should adopt agile marketing differently. Complicated structure and bureaucracy inherent in big organizations are the worst enemies of agile marketing. The companies need to set up separate teams to ensure they maintain stable and profitable operations while ensuring that they are not missing out on the next big thing.

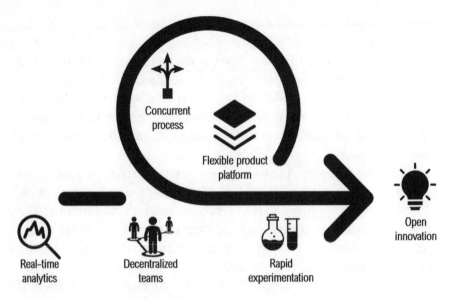

FIGURE 12.1 Developing Agile Marketing

Thus, the agile process is usually reserved only for innovation projects that focus on new growth engines.

There are several key components in an agile marketing organization (see Figure 12.1). First, businesses need to set up real-time analytics. The next is to establish decentralized agile teams that feed on the insights generated by the analytics. Then, the teams make multiple product or campaign configurations based on a flexible platform. They run rapid experimentation in a concurrent process from ideation to prototyping. Upon testing each configuration with real market acceptance analytics, they will determine which one brings the most favorable outcome. In conducting the entire agile process, companies must embrace an open innovation mentality in which companies leverage both internal and external resources.

Build a Real-Time Analytics Capability

Agile marketing has a quick response mechanism. The first thing to build, therefore, is the analytics capability. The objective is to identify problems that need solutions or opportunities for growth. For this purpose, businesses must have a customer data capture that monitors changes in real time. Social listening tools—also known as social media monitoring—can be particularly useful to track discussions about a brand or a product on social media and online communities. The tools filter unstructured social conversations into usable customer intelligence, such as keywords, emerging trends, polarizing opinions, brand sentiments, campaign visibility, product acceptance, and competitor response. The data is also enriched with geotagging, which allows companies to track insights by regions and locations.

Companies also need to track changes in customer behavior reflected by traffic and transactions. Companies can follow customer journeys on their websites and analyze e-commerce purchases in real time. For companies with physical assets, point of sales (POS) data are the most common to evaluate if a particular product SKU is getting traction from the market. Using RFID tags on products, companies can get a better picture of the pre-purchase customer journey. For instance, retailers can gain insight on how long it takes customers to decide before buying a product and the journey they take before the product gets to the cashiers.

With permission, RFID tags can also function as wearables to track customer movements and improve customer experience. Disney embeds RFID into Magic Bands to track visitor movements in its theme parks. The Mayo Clinic uses RFID on the patient's wristband and staff's badges for the same purpose. B2B companies use RFID tracking to manage logistics and optimize the supply chain.

These traffic and transaction data are useful to quickly analyze causality between campaigns and results, or between product launches and sales. In other areas, the goal is to find the best product–market fit. The metrics to measure success must be meaningful and actionable so that companies precisely know what to refine from the campaigns or products. The real-time analytics empowers companies to experiment and get validated learning quickly.

Establish Decentralized Teams

Agile marketing requires multiple small teams to work on different things. The teams will feed on the insights generated by real-time analytics. In agile marketing, each group is assigned to a specific task with a timeline to complete. Thus, the teams are more accountable. The model draws inspiration from the scrum—an agile method most commonly used for software development. In marketing space, the applications of the agile approach may include new customer experience (CX) design, product innovation, marketing process improvement, creative marketing campaign, and new business development.

One of the main hurdles of agile marketing is organizational silos. Many large organizations struggle to align different functions with conflicting key performance indicators (KPIs). Thus, each agile team should have dedicated cross-functional members with diverse expertise: product development, marketing, and technology. Since the groups are small and they work on the same sets of objectives, the silos can be eliminated. At the same time, employees are more engaged and feel that their work is meaningful.

Aside from reducing any friction, cross-functional teams are suited for divergent thinking, which is essential in any innovation project. Cross-functional teams are also compulsory to bring ideas to life. The marketing person, for instance, plays a role in interpreting insights while the engineering person helps develop working prototypes. Each team should have all the necessary resources to complete the objectives independently.

Traditional decision-making models with the multilayer approval process are also too cumbersome for agile marketing. Decisions need to be made quickly, and delays will impact the outcome significantly. Thus, the teams must be autonomous and empowered with decentralized decision-making authority related to their assignment. The flexible model requires strong top management commitment. The role of senior management in agile marketing is to monitor progress, give feedback at the strategic level, and coach the teams while providing the teams with freedom. But most importantly, top executives must integrate all agile projects and align them with the company's overall goals.

Develop a Flexible Product Platform

The most significant reason why agile teams have a fast turnaround is that they do not build new projects from scratch. Instead, every new iteration comes from the same base, which is called a platform. When customers evaluate a specific product, for instance, they do not love or hate it entirely. They might dislike some elements while desiring others. Thus, everything—product features, software components, CX touchpoints, or creative designs—is designed to be modular and layered. The base serves as the core product while other modules can be assembled differently on top to augment the product.

Software and other digital companies by default are more flexible and agile in their product development. With no physical assets, they can better adapt to market volatility and uncertainty. Despite its roots in digital products, the practice is also common in hardware companies. In automotive, for instance, it is common to base product development on only a few platforms. Different car models with distinct looks and even different automaker brands might use the same platform. The rationale for this practice is to save costs and standardize manufacturing processes globally. That way, automakers can keep prices low while still providing customized design variations catering to different market preferences.

In some cases, companies shift their business model from hardware ownership to digital services to improve their agility. Hardware and software products have longer sales cycles as customers do not frequently upgrade them if improvements are not significant. Thus, agile marketing might not be as useful. That is why tech companies move up from selling enterprise hardware and software to offering service subscriptions. With the new revenue model, they can provide products that are well integrated and continuously upgraded.

With the flexible product platform, agile teams can quickly experiment with various configurations until they gain the most favorable feedback from the market. But most importantly, product platforms and modular components enable companies to do mass customizations. Customers can choose their unique configurations for all kinds of products, such as frozen yogurt, shoes, and laptops.

Develop Concurrent Process

The innovation project typically follows a *waterfall* or stage-gate model, where every step from ideation to launch is done in sequence. There is a checkpoint at the end of each stage. Therefore, the process cannot move on to the next phase before the predecessor is complete. The multiple checkpoints make this approach time-consuming.

In agile marketing, the model is replaced by the concurrent method, in which different stages run in parallel. Aside from the apparent speed, the concurrent process has another major benefit. The waterfall model is not suitable for large-scale and long-term projects in which mistakes discovered late in the process could mean restarting the whole sequence. The structured model is also very rigid and does not allow for significant alterations once the project kicks off. The concurrent process is the solution to these issues.

Since it is not sequential, every component of innovation—design, production, business case—is taken into consideration early in the process. Work is also broken down into small workstreams with short milestones. Thus, potential problems can be identified and fixed before the innovation is already too deep into the development.

But the concurrent process also poses some challenges to overcome. The most significant risk is during the integration between workstreams. Constant coordination within and between teams is critical to make sure the workstreams are aligned and compatible. Every incremental progress and change in one workstream must be communicated so that adjustments can be made in other workstreams. Agile teams must conduct a short daily meeting for this coordination purpose. Since the meeting is brief, they must make decisions quickly. Those that are new to agile might find it challenging to do so.

In agile marketing, development phases are also done concurrently with experimentation. The teams will never wait for the market testing of a recently completed iteration. Instead, they continue to move on with the next iteration. Hence, to influence the subsequent development, the market test must be conducted rapidly in between iterations.

Perform Rapid Experimentation

Rapid experimentation is one of the most important elements of agile marketing. Traditionally, concept testing relies on pre-launch market research. The pre-launch study focuses on discovering customer insights, which become the basis for new product development or campaign ideas. The ideas are then presented to a group of respondents during concept tests. Since the concepts are still hypothetical, and often without working prototypes, the respondents have difficulty imagining the final products. Hence, the concept test could be biased. Moreover, there is usually a delay before the results come in—making it too late to make alterations.

In agile marketing, however, actual products are produced in small batches and sold to real customers based on the lean startup playbook. The early product version with just enough features for launch is called the minimum viable product (MVP). It is important to note the definition of *product* is broad, which may include an actual product, a new UI/UX, or a campaign idea. It is essential to launch the MVP as quickly as possible so that companies can get first learning for future enhancement and augmentation of the product.

Rapid experimentation enables businesses to learn in a controlled environment. The experiments are isolated to specific geographical locations so that companies can safely contain failures and manage risks. Several iterations can be made to refine the product continuously over time. Moreover, real-time analytics allows companies to measure market acceptance instantly before the launch of the next version or the bigger rollout.

In conducting experiments, it is not always about persevering with the original ideas and making continuous, small improvements. In some cases, market acceptance is so poor for several iterations that the agile team must decide to change the project course radically. Newfound insights coming from the analytics could also change the direction of the project. In agile, this is known as pivoting. Pivoting is challenging because the team must go back to the drawing board and rethink the problems or opportunities. The ability to quickly pivot when things do not go their way is often considered the biggest difference between traditional and agile organizations.

Embrace Open Innovation

Despite being centered around teams, the agile approach does not mean that companies must do everything in-house. To cut time to market, companies must leverage both internal and external resources. The concept of *open innovation*—a term introduced by Henry Chesbrough—is aligned with agile marketing. The approach gives companies access to a global pool of ideas, solutions, and specialist talents. Moreover, with this model, companies do not need to build their innovation labs or research and development centers, which have a higher cost structure.

Today, businesses open up their innovation process, using both inside-out and outside-in approaches. Major companies open-source the technologies that they have created behind closed doors to the outside world. That way a worldwide community of developers can build on those technologies and return the improvements to the source. Google, for example, has open-sourced TensorFlow, its advanced artificial intelligence (AI) engine.

Businesses have also accepted ideas from outside networks. Customer co-creation and third-party collaboration are proven to accelerate and improve the quality of innovation. There are several ways companies can embrace external ideas. The most common is the open innovation challenge. Companies can publicly post the challenges they face and request for solutions. Singapore Airlines seeks for digital solutions that redefine its customer experience via the AppChallenge. Zurich Innovation Championship looks for technology ideas for the insurance sector, which include AI and natural language processing (NLP) applications.

Another way to gather external solutions is via an open innovation marketplace. One such platform is InnoCentive, which serves as the bridge between innovation seekers and a network of solvers for cash rewards. Companies can also build their network of external innovation partners. A prominent example is P&G's Connect+Develop, a platform that helps the company to manage partnerships with innovators and patent holders.

The biggest challenge of using the open innovation model is aligning the agile teams and the innovation partners. Agile teams are typically co-located to ensure close collaboration in a limited time. The open innovation requires agile teams to collaborate with external parties, making it a distributed agile model.

Agile Marketing Project Management

The application of agile principles in marketing project management requires quick and concise documentation. A one-page worksheet helps agile teams to wrap their minds around specific marketing projects (see Figure 12.2). Since coordination is critical in the agile system, the document is also a communication tool to convey incremental progress made in every cycle.

The worksheet must contain several essential elements. The first is the market requirements section, which lays out the problems to solve and the opportunities for improvement based on real-time data. Proposed solutions and iterations must also be well documented, especially the minimum viable product definition. The worksheet should also contain essential tasks with the timeline and person in charge. Finally, it must also

AGILE MARKETING WORKSHEET

Marketing Initiative	Revamp CX for sales touchpoints	Team

Team
Bill (Sales Dept.)
Lea (Customer Service Dept.)
John (Marketing Dept.)
Arianna (Telemarketing Dept.)
Taylor (IT Dept.)

Workstream	Develop lead generation chatbot

Cycle	1.0	Timeline	July Week 1-4

Market Requirements

CUSTOMER PROBLEM
- Average response time for website inquiries: 48 hours

INTERNAL PROBLEM
- Inbound inquiries per month: 5,000
- Admin staff: 2
- Qualified leads per month: 500
- Inquiry types: 58% product-related, 11% demo request

Solutions/Improvements

MINIMUM VIABLE PRODUCT
- Based on existing chatbot builder platform
- Conversational chatbot with instant response
- Able to respond to 50% of product-related inquiries

KEY GOALS & METRICS
- Unique chatbot users in first month: 1,000
- Number of qualified leads in first month: 200

Tasks	When	Who
Compare and select platform	Week 1	Taylor
Develop FAQ responses	Week 1-2	Bill
Design conversation flow	Week 2-3	Lea
Create storyboards	Week 2-3	John
Build beta version	Week 3-4	Taylor
Deploy the beta version	Week 4	Taylor

Market Testing Results

KEY GOALS & METRICS
- Unique chatbot users in 1st month: 500
- Number of qualified leads in 1st month: 50

FEEDBACK
- Chatbot placement on website not prominent; visitors are not aware of chatbot
- Average interactions per user: 2.3; add this to Key Goals & Metrics
- Need to add more use cases with automated demo scheduling as next priority

FIGURE 12.2   Agile Marketing Worksheet Example

document the market testing results, which will be useful for the next iteration.

The worksheet must be written for every cycle or iteration and distributed to all related parties. But the documentation process never becomes a paperwork burden for the team. The purpose is to align objectives with the actions and results in every marketing project.

Summary: Executing Marketing Initiatives at Pace and Scale

Across industries, the product lifecycles are shortening, driven by the constant change in customer expectations and the proliferation of new products. The phenomenon is also happening in the customer experience, which can become obsolete in a short period.

Traditional models of marketing planning and project management do not fit the new landscape. The long-term marketing strategy is no longer relevant. The waterfall or stage-gate approach to innovation is considered too slow. The always-on customers demand that companies keep up with organization flexibility, which calls for an agile marketing approach. Operational stability must also be complemented by agile marketing, which becomes the catalyst for growth.

An agile marketing execution requires several components. Real-time analytics allows companies to capture market insights quickly. Based on the newly discovered ideas, marketing initiatives are designed and developed in small batches and incremental fashion by decentralized agile teams. The teams utilize a flexible platform and concurrent process to come up with a minimum viable product. The product iteration is then tested via rapid experimentation. To speed up the process even further, companies may embrace open innovation and leverage both internal and external resources.

REFLECTION QUESTIONS

- Evaluate the agility of your organization. What are the obstacles to implementing agile marketing in your organization?
- What are marketing initiatives that you can design and develop using agile marketing in your organization? Apply all the components and use the agile marketing worksheet.

Index